MISS SANTA CLAUS
OF THE PULLMAN

Miss Santa Claus

MISS SANTA CLAUS OF THE PULLMAN

BY
ANNIE FELLOWS JOHNSON
Author of "The Little Colonel Series," etc.

With illustrations by
REGINALD B. BIRCH

NEW YORK
THE CENTURY CO.
1913

Copyright, 1913, by
The Century Co.

Published, October, 1913

TO
MY SISTERS
LURA AND ALBION

LIST OF ILLUSTRATIONS

Miss Santa Claus . . . . *Frontispiece*

                                                  PAGE

"Oh, dear Santa Claus" 19

"Here!" he said 29

"Oh, rabbit *dravy!*" he cried 57

He pushed aside the red plush curtain and looked in 69

And ran after the boy as hard as she could go . 77

It was about the Princess Ina 99

The shower of stars falling on the blanket made her think of the star-flower 121

"Take it back!" 165

MISS SANTA CLAUS OF
THE PULLMAN

MISS SANTA CLAUS OF THE PULLMAN

CHAPTER I

THE last half hour had seemed endless to Will'm, almost as long as the whole four years of his life. With his stubby little shoes drawn up under him, and his soft bobbed hair flapping over his ears every time the rockers tilted forward, he sat all alone in the sitting-room behind the shop, waiting and rocking.

It seemed as if everybody at the Junction wanted something that afternoon; thread or buttons or yarn, or the home-made doughnuts which helped out the slim stock of goods in the little notion store which had once been the parlor. And it seemed as if

MISS SANTA CLAUS

Grandma Neal never would finish waiting on the customers and come back to tell the rest of the story about the Camels and the Star; for no sooner did one person go out than another one came in. He knew by the tinkling of the bell over the front door, every time it opened or shut.

The door between the shop and sitting-room being closed, Will'm could not hear much that was said, but several times he caught the word "Christmas," and once somebody said *"Santa Claus,"* in such a loud happy-sounding voice that he slipped down from the chair and ran across the room to open the door a crack. It was only lately that he had begun to hear much about Santa Claus. Not until Libby started to school that fall did they know that there is such a wonderful person in the world. Of course they had heard his name, as they had heard Jack Frost's, and had seen his picture in story-books and advertisements, but they hadn't known that he is really true till the other children told Libby. Now nearly

OF THE PULLMAN

every day she came home with something new she had learned about him.

Will'm must have known always about Christmas though, for he still had a piece of a rubber dog which his father had sent him on his first one, and—a Teddy Bear on his second. And while he could n't recall anything about those first two festivals except what Libby told him, he could remember the last one perfectly. There had been a sled, and a fire-engine that wound up with a key, and Grandma Neal had made him some cooky soldiers with red cinnamon-drop buttons on their coats.

She was n't his own grandmother, but she had taken the place of one to Libby and him, all the years he had been in the world. Their father paid their board, to be sure, and sent them presents and came to see them at long intervals when he could get away from his work, but that was so seldom that Will'm did not feel very well acquainted with him; not so well as Libby did. She was three years older, and could even remember a little bit about their mother before she went off to heaven to get well. Mrs. Neal was n't like a real grandmother in many ways. She was almost too young, for one thing. She was always very brisk and very busy, and, as she frequently remarked, she meant what she said and *she would be minded*.

That is why Will'm turned the knob so softly that no one noticed for a moment that the door was ajar. A black-bearded man in a rough overcoat was examining a row of dolls which dangled by their necks from a line above the show case. He was saying jokingly:

"Well, Mrs. Neal, I 'll have to be buying some of these jimcracks before long. If this mud keeps up, no reindeer living could get out to my place, and it would n't do for the young'uns to be disappointed Christmas morning."

Then he caught sight of a section of a small boy peeping through the door, for all that showed of Will'm through the crack

OF THE PULLMAN

was a narrow strip of blue overalls which covered him from neck to ankles, a round pink cheek and one solemn eye peering out from under his thatch of straight flaxen hair like a little Skye terrier's. When the man saw that eye he hurried to say: "Of course mud ought n't to make any difference to *Santy's* reindeer. They take the *Sky Road,* right over the house tops and all."

The crack widened till two eyes peeped in, shining with interest, and both stubby shoes ventured over the threshold. A familiar sniffle made Grandma Neal turn around.

"Go back to the fire, William," she said briskly. "It is n't warm enough in here for you with that cold of yours."

The order was obeyed as promptly as it was given, but with a bang of the door so rebellious and unexpected that the man laughed. There was an amused expression on the woman's face, too, as she glanced up from the package she was tying, to explain with an indulgent smile.

"That was n't all temper, Mr. Woods. It was part embarrassment that made him slam the door. Usually he does n't mind strangers, but he takes spells like that sometimes."

"That 's only natural," was the drawling answer. "But it is n't everybody who knows how to manage children, Mrs. Neal. I hope now that his stepmother when he gets her, will understand him as well as you do. My wife tells me that the poor little kids are going to have one soon. How do they take to the notion?"

Mrs. Neal stiffened a little at the question, although he was an old friend, and his interest was natural under the circumstances. There was a slight pause, then she said:

"I have n't mentioned the subject to them yet. No use to make them cross their bridge before they get to it. I 've no doubt Molly will be good to them. She was a nice little thing when she used to go to school here at the Junction."

OF THE PULLMAN

"It's queer," mused the man, "how she and Bill Branfield used to think so much of each other, from their First Reader days till both families moved away from here, and then that they should come across each other after all these years, from different states, too."

Instinctively they had lowered their voices, but Will'm on the other side of the closed door was making too much noise of his own to hear anything they were saying. Lying full length on the rug in front of the fire, he battered his heels up and down on the floor and pouted. His cold made him miserable, and being sent out of the shop made him cross. If he had been allowed to stay there's no telling what he might have heard about those reindeer to repeat to Libby when she came home from school.

Suddenly Will'm remembered the last bit of information which she had brought home to him, and, scrambling hastily up from the floor, he climbed into the rocking chair as if something were after him:

MISS SANTA CLAUS

"Santa Claus is apt to be looking down the chimney any minute to see how you're behaving. And no matter if your lips don't show it outside, he knows when you're all puckered up with crossness and pouting on the inside!"

At that terrible thought Will'm began to rock violently back and forth and sing. It was a choky, sniffling little tune that he sang. His voice sounded thin and far away even to his own ears, because his cold was so bad. But the thought that Santa might be listening, and would write him down as a good little boy, kept him valiantly at it for several minutes. Then because he had a way of chanting his thoughts out loud sometimes, instead of thinking them to himself, he went on, half chanting, half talking the story of the Camels and the Star, which he was waiting for Grandma Neal to come back and finish. He knew it as well as she did, because she had told it to him so often in the last week.

"An' the wise men rode through the night,

OF THE PULLMAN

an' they rode an' they rode, an' the bells on the bridles went ting-a-ling! just like the bell on Dranma's shop door. An' the drate big Star shined down on 'em and went ahead to show 'em the way. An' the drate big reindeer runned along the Sky Road"—he was mixing Grandma Neal's story now with what he had heard through the crack in the door, and he found the mixture much more thrilling than the original recital. "An' they runned an' they runned an' the sleighbells went ting-a-ling! just like the bell on Dranma's shop door. An' after a long time they all comed to the house where the baby king was at. Nen the wise men jumped off their camels and knelt down and opened all their boxes of pretty things for Him to play with. An' the reindeer knelt down on the roof where the drate big shining star stood still, so Santy could empty all his pack down the baby king's chimney."

It was a queer procession which wandered through Will'm's sniffling, sing-song account. To the camels, sages and herald

MISS SANTA CLAUS

angels, to the shepherds and the little woolly white lambs of the Judean hills, were added not only Bo Peep and her flock, but Baa the black sheep, and the reindeer team of an unscriptural Saint Nicholas. But it was all Holy Writ to Will'm. Presently the mere thought of angels and stars and silver bells gave him such a big warm feeling inside, that he was brimming over with good-will to everybody.

When Libby came home from school a few minutes later, he was in the midst of his favorite game, one which he played at intervals all through the day. The game was Railroad Train, suggested naturally enough by the constant switching of cars and snorting of engines which went on all day and night at this busy Junction. It was one in which he could be a star performer in each part, as he personated fireman, engineer, conductor and passenger in turn. At the moment Libby came in he was the engine itself, backing, puffing and whistling, his arms going like piston-rods, and his pursed

OF THE PULLMAN

up little mouth giving a very fair imitation of "letting off steam."

"Look out!" he called warningly. "You'll get runned over."

But instead of heeding his warning, Libby planted herself directly in the path of the oncoming engine, ignoring so completely the part he was playing that he stopped short in surprise. Ordinarily she would have fallen in with the game, but now she seemed blind and deaf to the fact that he was playing anything at all. Usually, coming in the back way, she left her muddy overshoes on the latticed porch, her lunch basket on the kitchen table, her wraps on their particular hook in the entry. She was an orderly little soul. But to-day she came in, her coat half off, her hood trailing down her back by its strings, and her thin little tails of tightly braided hair fuzzy and untied, from running bare-headed all the way home to tell the exciting news. She told it in gasps.

"You can write letters to Santa Claus—for whatever you want—and put them up

MISS SANTA CLAUS

the chimney—and he gets them—and whatever you ask for he'll bring you—if you're good!"

Instantly the engine was a little boy again all a-tingle with this new delicious mystery of Christmastide. He climbed up into the rocking chair and listened, the rapt look on his face deepening. In proof of what she told, Libby had a letter all written and addressed, ready to send. One of the older girls had helped her with it at noon, and she had spent the entire afternoon recess copying it. Because she was just learning to write, she made so many mistakes that it had to be copied several times. She read it aloud to Will'm.

"Dear Santa Claus:—Please bring me a little shiny gold ring like the one that Maudie Peters wears. Yours truly, Libby Branfield."

"Now you watch, and you'll see me send it up the chimney when I get my muddy overshoes off and my hands washed. This might be one of the times when he'd be

OF THE PULLMAN

looking down, and it'd be better for me to be all clean and tidy."

Breathlessly Will'm waited till she came back from the kitchen, her hands and face shining from the scrubbing she had given them with yellow laundry soap, her hair brushed primly back on each side of its parting and her hair ribbons freshly tied. Then she knelt on the rug, the fateful missive in her hand.

"Maudie is going to ask for 'most a dozen presents," she said. "But as long as this will be Santy's first visit to this house I'm not going to ask for more than one thing, and you mustn't either. It wouldn't be polite."

"But we can ask him to bring a ring to Dranma," Will'm suggested, his face beaming at the thought. The answer was positive and terrible out of her wisdom newly gained at both church and school.

"No, we can't! He only brings things to people who *bleeve* in him. It's the same way it is about going to Heaven. Only

MISS SANTA CLAUS

those who *bleeve* will be saved and get in."

"Dranma and Uncle Neal will go to Heaven," insisted Will'm loyally, and in a tone which suggested his willingness to hurt her if she contradicted him. Uncle Neal was "Dranma's" husband.

"Oh, of course, they'll go to *Heaven* all right," was Libby's impatient answer. "They've got faith in the Bible and the minister and the heathen and such things. But they won't get anything in their stockings because they are n't sure about there even *being* a Santa Claus! So there!"

"Well, if Santa Claus won't put anything in my Dranma Neal's stocking, he's a mean old thing, and I don't want him to put anything in mine," began Will'm defiantly, but was silenced by the sight of Libby's horrified face.

"Oh, brother! *"Hush!"* she cried, darting a frightened glance over her shoulder towards the chimney. Then in a shocked whisper which scared Will'm worse than a

OF THE PULLMAN

loud yell would have done, she said impressively, "Oh, I *hope* he has n't heard you! He never would come to this house as long as he lives! And I could n't *bear* for us to find just empty stockings Christmas morning."

There was a tense silence. And then, still on her knees, her hands still clasped over the letter, she moved a few inches nearer the fireplace. The next instant Will'm heard her call imploringly up the chimney, "Oh, dear Santa Claus, if you 're up there looking down, *please* don't mind what Will'm said. He 's so little he does n't know any better. *Please* forgive him and send us what we ask for, for Jesus' sake, Amen!"

Fascinated, Will'm watched the letter flutter up past the flames, drawn by the strong draught of the flue. Then suddenly shamed by the thought that he had been publicly prayed for, *out loud and in the daytime,* he ran to cast himself on the old lounge, face downward among the cushions.

MISS SANTA CLAUS

Libby herself felt a trifle constrained after her unusual performance, and to cover her embarrassment seized the hearth broom and vigorously swept up the scraps of half-dried mud which she had tracked in a little while before. Then she stood and drummed on the window pane a long time, looking out into the dusk which always came so surprisingly fast these short winter days, almost the very moment after the sun dropped down behind the cedar trees.

It was a relief to both children when Grandma Neal came in with a lighted lamp. Her cheerful call to know who was going to help her set the supper table, gave Will'm an excuse to spring up from the lounge cushions and face his little world once more in a natural and matter-of-course way. He felt safer out in the bright warm kitchen. No stern displeased eye could possibly peer at him around the bend of that black shining stove-pipe. There was comfort in the savory steam puffing out from under the lid of the stew-pan on the stove. There was

"Oh, dear Santa Claus"

OF THE PULLMAN

reassurance in the clatter of the knives and forks and dishes which he and Libby put noisily in place on the table. But when Grandma Neal started where she had left off, to finish the story of the Camels and the Star, he interrupted quickly to ask instead for the tale of Goldilocks and the Three Bears. The Christmas Spirit had gone out of him. He could not listen to the story of the Star. It lighted the way not only of the camel caravan, but of the Sky Road too, and he did n't want to be reminded of that Sky Road now. He was fearful that a cold displeasure might be filling the throat of the sitting-room chimney. If Santa Claus *had* happened to be listening when he called him a mean old thing, then had he ruined not only his own chances, but Libby's too. That fear followed him all evening. It made him vaguely uncomfortable. Even when they sat down to supper it did something to his appetite, for the dumpling stew did not taste as good as usual.

CHAPTER II

IT was several days before Will'm lost that haunting fear of having displeased the great power up the chimney past all forgiveness. It began to leave him gradually as Libby grew more and more sure of her own state of favor. She was so good in school now that even the teacher said nobody could be better, no matter how hard he tried. She stayed every day to help clean the blackboards and collect the pencils. She never missed a syllable nor stepped off the line in spelling class, nor asked for a drink in lesson time. And she and Maudie Peters had made it up between them not to whisper a single word until after Christmas. She was sure now that even if Santa Claus had overheard Will'm, her explanation that he was too little to know any better had made it all right.

MISS SANTA CLAUS

It is probable, too, that Will'm's state of body helped his state of mind, for about this time his cold was well enough for him to play out of doors, and the thought of stars and angels and silver bells began to be agreeable again. They gave him that big, warm feeling inside again; the Christmas feeling of good-will to everybody.

One morning he was sitting up on a post of the side yard fence, when the passenger train Number Four came rushing in to the station, and was switched back on a side track right across the road from him. It was behind time and had to wait there for orders or till the Western Flyer passed it, or for some such reason. It was a happy morning for Will'm. There was nothing he enjoyed so much as having one of these long Pullman trains stop where he could watch it. Night after night he and Libby had flattened their faces against the sitting-room window to watch the seven o'clock limited pass by. Through its brilliantly lighted windows they loved to see the passengers at

MISS SANTA CLAUS

dinner. The white tables with their gleam of glass and shine of silver and glow of shaded lights seemed wonderful to them More wonderful still was it to be eating as unconcernedly as if one were at home, with the train jiggling the tables while it leaped across the country at its highest speed. The people who could do such things must be wonderful too.

There were times when passengers flattening *their* faces against the glass to see why the train had stopped, caught the gleam of a cheerful home window across the road, and holding shielding hands at either side of their eyes, as they peered through the darkness, smiled to discover those two eager little watchers, who counted the stopping of the Pullman at this Junction as the greatest event of the day.

Will'm and Libby knew nearly every engineer and conductor on the road by sight, and had their own names for them. The engineer on this morning train they called Mr. Smiley, because he always had a cheer-

OF THE PULLMAN

ful grin for them, and sometimes a wave of his big grimy hand. This time Mr. Smiley was too busy and too provoked by the delay to pay any attention to the small boy perched on the fence post. Some of the passengers finding that they might have to wait half an hour or more began to climb out and walk up and down the road past him. Several of them attracted by the wares in the window of the little notion shop which had once been a parlor, sauntered in and came out again, eating some of Grandma Neal's doughnuts. Presently Will'm noticed that everybody who passed a certain sleeping coach, stooped down and looked under it. He felt impelled to look under it himself and discover why. So he climbed down from the post and trudged along the road, kicking the rocks out of his way with stubby little shoes already scuffed from much previous kicking. At the same moment the steward of the dining-car stepped down from the vestibuled platform, and strolled towards him, with his hands in his trousers' pockets.

MISS SANTA CLAUS

"Hullo, son!" he remarked good-humoredly in passing, giving an amused glance at the solemn child stuffed into a gray sweater and blue mittens, with a toboggan cap pulled down over his soft bobbed hair. Usually Will'm responded to such greetings. So many people came into the shop that he was not often abashed by strangers. But this time he was so busy looking at something that dangled from the steward's vest pocket that he failed to say "Hullo" back at him. It was what seemed to be the smallest gold watch he had ever seen, and it impressed him as very queer that the man should wear it on the outside of his pocket instead of the inside. He stopped still in the road and stared at it until the man passed him, then he turned and followed him slowly at a distance.

A few rods further on, the steward stooped and looked under the coach, and spoke to a man who was out of sight, but who was hammering on the other side. A voice called back something about a hot-box and cutting

OF THE PULLMAN

out that coach, and reminded of his original purpose, Will'm followed on and looked, likewise. Although he squatted down and looked for a long time he could n't see a single box, only the legs of the man who was hammering on the other side. But just as he straightened up again he caught the gleam of something round and shiningly golden, something no bigger than a quarter, lying almost between his feet. It was a tiny baby watch like the one that swung from the steward's vest pocket.

Thrilled by the discovery, Will'm picked it up and fondled it with both little blue mittens. It did n't tick when he held it to his ear, and he could n't open it, but he was sure that Uncle Neal could open it and start it to going, and he was sure that it was the littlest watch in the world. It never occurred to him that finding it had n't made it his own to have and to carry home, just like the rainbow-lined mussel shells that he sometimes picked up on the creek bank, or the silver dime he had once found in a wagon rut.

MISS SANTA CLAUS

Then he looked up to see the steward strolling back towards him again, his hands still in his trousers' pockets. But this time no fascinating baby watch bobbed back and forth against his vest as he walked, and Will'm knew with a sudden stab of disappointment that was as bad as earache, that the watch he was fondling could never be his to carry home and show proudly to Uncle Neal. It belonged to the man.

"Here!" he said, holding it out in the blue mitten.

"Well, I vow!" exclaimed the steward, looking down at his watchfob, and then snatching the little disk of gold from the outstretched hand. "I would n't have lost that for hardly anything. It must have come loose when I stooped to look under the car. I think more of that than almost anything I 've got. See?"

And then Will'm saw that it was not a watch, but a little locket made to hang from a bar that was fastened to a wide black ribbon fob. The man pulled out the fob, and

"Here!" he said

OF THE PULLMAN

there on the other end, where it had been in his pocket all the time, was a big watch, as big as Will'm's fist. The locket flew open when he touched a spring, and there were two pictures inside. One of a lady and one of a jolly, fat-cheeked baby.

"Well, little man!" exclaimed the steward, with a hearty clap on the shoulder that nearly upset him. "You don't know how big a favor you 've done me by finding that locket. You 're just about the nicest boy I 've come across yet. I 'll have to tell Santa Claus about you. What 's your name?"

Will'm told him and pointed across to the shop, when asked where he lived. At the steward's high praise Will'm was ready to take the Sky Road himself, when he heard that he was to be reported to the Master of the Reindeer as the nicest boy the steward had come across. His disappointment vanished so quickly that he even forgot that he had been disappointed, and when the steward caught him under the arms and swung

MISS SANTA CLAUS

him up the steps, saying something about finding an orange, he was thrilled with a wild brave sense of adventure.

Discovering that Will'm had never been on a Pullman since he could remember, the steward took him through the diner to the kitchen, showing him all the sights and explaining all the mysteries. It was as good as a show to watch the child's face. He had never dreamed that such roasting and broiling went on in the narrow space of the car kitchen, or that such quantities of eatables were stored away in the mammoth refrigerators which stood almost touching the red hot ranges. Big shining fish from far-off waters, such as the Junction had never heard of, lay blocked in ice in one compartment. Ripe red strawberries lay in another, although it was mid December, and in Will'm's part of the world strawberries were not to be thought of before the first of June. There were more eggs than all the hens at the Junction could lay in a week, and a white-capped, white-jacketed colored-man

OF THE PULLMAN

was beating up a dozen or so into a white mountain of meringue, which the passengers would eat by and by in the shape of some strange, delicious dessert, sitting at those fascinating tables he had passed on his way in.

A quarter of an hour later when Will'm found himself on the ground again, gazing after the departing train, he was a trifle dazed with all he had seen and heard. But three things were clear in his mind. That he held in one hand a great yellow orange, in the other a box of prize pop-corn, and in his heart the precious assurance that Santa Claus would be told by one in high authority that he was a good boy.

So elated was he by this last fact, that he decided on the way home to send a letter up the chimney on his own account, especially as he knew now exactly what to ask for. He had been a bit hazy on the question before. Now he knew beyond all doubt that what he wanted more than anything in the wide world, was *a ride on a Pullman car*.

MISS SANTA CLAUS

He wanted to sit at one of those tables, and eat things that had been cooked in that mysterious kitchen, at the same time that he was flying along through the night on the wings of a mighty dragon breathing out smoke and fire as it flew.

He went in to the house by way of the shop so that he might make the bell go ting-a-ling. It was so delightfully like the bells on the camels, also like the bells on the sleigh which would be coming before so very long to bring him what he wanted.

Miss Sally Watts was sitting behind the counter, crocheting. To his question of "Where's Dranma?" she answered without looking up.

"She and Mr. Neal have driven over to Westfield. They have some business at the court house. She said you're not to go off the place again till she gets back. I was to tell you when you came in. She looked everywhere to find you before she left, because she's going to be gone till late in the afternoon. Where you been, anyhow?"

OF THE PULLMAN

Will'm told her. Miss Sally was a neighbor who often helped in the shop at times like this, and he was always glad when such times came. It was easy to tell Miss Sally things, and presently when a few direct questions disclosed the fact that Miss Sally "bleeved" as he did, he asked her another question, which had been puzzling him ever since he had decided to ask for a ride on the train.

"How can Santa put a *ride* in a *stocking?*"

"I don't know," answered Miss Sally, still intent on her crocheting. "But then I don't really see how he can put anything in; sleds or dolls or anything of the sort. He's a mighty mysterious man to me. But then, probably he would n't try to put the *ride* in a stocking. He'd send the ticket or the money to buy it with. And he *might* give it to you beforehand, and not wait for stocking-hanging time, knowing how much you want it."

All this from Miss Sally because Mrs.

MISS SANTA CLAUS

Neal had just told her that the children were to be sent to their father the day before Christmas, and that they were to go on a Pullman car, because the ordinary coaches did not go straight through. The children were too small to risk changing cars, and he was too busy to come for them.

Will'm stayed in the shop the rest of the morning, for Miss Sally echoing the sentiment of everybody at the Junction, felt sorry for the poor little fellow who was soon to be sent away to a stepmother, and felt that it was her duty to do what she could toward making his world as pleasant as possible for him, while she had the opportunity.

Together they ate the lunch which had been left on the pantry shelves for them. Will'm helped set it out on the table. Then he went back into the shop with Miss Sally. But his endless questions "got on her nerves" after awhile, she said, and she suddenly ceased to be the good company that she had been all morning. She mended the fire in the sitting-room and told Will'm he'd

OF THE PULLMAN

better play in there till Libby came home. It was an endless afternoon, so long that after he had done everything that he could think of to pass the time, he decided he'd write his own letter and send it up the chimney himself. He could n't possibly wait for Libby to come home and do it. He'd write a picture letter. It was easier to read pictures than print, anyhow. At least for him. He slipped back into the shop long enough to get paper and a pencil from the old secretary in the corner, and then lying on his stomach on the hearth-rug with his heels in the air, he began drawing his favorite sketch, a train of cars.

All that can be said of the picture is that one could recognize what it was meant for. The wheels were wobbly and no two of the same size, the windows zigzagged in uneven lines and were of varied shapes. The cowcatcher looked as if it could toss anything it might pick up high enough to join the cow that jumped over the moon. But it was unmistakably a train, and the long line of

MISS SANTA CLAUS

smoke pouring back over it from the tipsy smoke-stack showed that it was going at the top of its speed. Despite the straggling scratchy lines any art critic must acknowledge that it had in it that intangible quality known as life and "go."

It puzzled Will'm at first to know how to introduce himself into the picture so as to show that he was the one wanting a ride. Finally on top of one of the cars he drew a figure supposed to represent a boy, and after long thought, drew one just like it, except that the second figure wore a skirt. He did n't want to take the ride alone. He'd be almost afraid to go without Libby, and he knew very well that she 'd like to go. She 'd often played "S'posen" they were riding away off to the other side of the world on one of those trains which they watched nightly pass the sitting-room window.

He wished he could spell his name and hers. He know only the letters with which each began, and he was n't sure of either unless he could see the picture on the other

OF THE PULLMAN

side of the building block on which it was printed. The box of blocks was in the sitting-room closet. He brought it out, emptied it on the rug and searched until he found the block bearing the picture of a lion. That was the king of beasts, and the L on the other side which stood for Lion, stood also for Libby. Very slowly and painstakingly he copied the letter on his drawing, placing it directly across the girl's skirt so that there could be no mistake. Then he pawed over the blocks till he found the one with the picture of a whale. That was the king of fishes, and the W on the other side which stood for Whale, stood also for William. He tried putting the W across the boy, but as each leg was represented by one straight line only, bent at right angles at the bottom to make a foot, the result was confusing. He rubbed out the legs, made them anew, and put the W over the boy's head, drawing a thin line from the end of the W to the crossed scratches representing fingers. That plainly showed that the Boy and the

MISS SANTA CLAUS

W were one and the same, although it gave to the unenlightened the idea that the picture had something to do with flying a kite. Then he rubbed out the L on Libby's skirt and placed it over her head, likewise connecting her letter with her fingers.

The rubbing-out process gave a smudgy effect. Will'm was not satisfied with the result, and like a true artist who counts all labor as naught, which helps him towards that perfection which is his ideal, he laid aside the drawing as unworthy and began another.

The second was better. He accomplished it with a more certain touch and with no smudges, and filled with the joy of a creator, sat and looked at it a few minutes before starting it on its flight up the flue towards the Sky Road.

The great moment was over. He had just drawn back from watching it start when Libby came in. She came primly and quietly this time. She had waited to leave her overshoes on the porch, her lunch basket

OF THE PULLMAN

in the kitchen, her wraps in the entry. The white ruffled apron which she had worn all day was scarcely mussed. The bows on her narrow braids stuck out stiffly and properly. Her shoes were tied and the laces tucked in. She walked on tiptoe, and every movement showed that she was keeping up the reputation she had earned of being "so good that nobody could be any better, no matter how hard he tried." She had been that good for over a week.

Will'm ran to get the orange which had been given him that morning. He had been saving it for this moment of division. He had already opened the pop-corn box and found the prize, a little china cup no larger than a thimble, and had used it at lunch, dipping a sip at a time from his glass of milk.

The interest with which she listened to his account of finding the locket and being taken aboard the train made him feel like a hero. He hastened to increase her respect.

"Nen the man said that I was about the nicest little boy he ever saw and he would

MISS SANTA CLAUS

tell Santa Claus so. An' I knew everything was all right so I've just sended a letter up to tell him to please give me a ride on the Pullman train."

Libby smiled in an amused, big-sister sort of way, asking how Will'm supposed anybody could read his letters. He couldn't write anything but scratches.

"But it was a picture letter!" Will'm explained triumphantly. "Anybody can read picture letters." Then he proceeded to tell what he had made and how he had marked it with the initials of the Lion and the Whale.

To his intense surprise Libby looked first startled, then troubled, then despairing. His heart seemed to drop down into his shoes when she exclaimed in a tragic tone:

"Well, Will'm Branfield! If you haven't gone and done it! I don't know what ever *is* going to happen to us *now!*"

Then she explained. *She* had already written a letter for him, with Susie Peters's help, asking in writing what she had asked

OF THE PULLMAN

before by word of mouth, that he be forgiven, and requesting that he might not find his stocking empty on Christmas morning. As to what should be in it, she had left that to Santa's generosity, because Will'm had never said what he wanted.

"And now," she added reproachfully, "I've *told* you that we ought n't to ask for more than one thing apiece, 'cause this is the first time he's ever been to this house, and it does n't seem polite to ask for so much from a stranger."

Will'm defended himself, his chin tilted at an angle that should have been a warning to one who could read such danger signals.

"I only asked for one thing for me and one for you."

"Yes, but don't you see, *I* had already asked for something for each of us, so that makes two things apiece," was the almost tearful answer.

"Well, *I* are n't to blame," persisted Will'm, "you did n't tell me what you'd done."

MISS SANTA CLAUS

"But you ought to have waited and asked me before you sent it," insisted Libby.

"I ought n't!"

"You *ought,* I say!" This with a stamp of her foot for emphasis.

"I ought n't, Miss Smarty!" This time a saucy little tongue thrust itself out at her from Will'm's mouth, and his face was screwed into the ugliest twist he could make.

Again he had the shock of a great surprise, when Libby did not answer with a worse face. Instead she lifted her head a little, and said in a voice almost honey-sweet, but so loud that it seemed intended for other ears than Will'm's, "Very well, have your own way, brother, but Santa Claus knows that *I* did n't want to be greedy and ask for two things!"

William answered in what was fairly a shout, "An' he knows that *I* did n't, *neether!*"

The shout was followed by a whisper: "Say, Libby, do you s'pose he heard that?"

Libby's answer was a convincing nod.

CHAPTER III

AFTER spending several days wondering how she could best break the news to the children that their father was going to take them away, Mrs. Neal decided that she would wait until the last possible moment. Then she would tell them that their father had a Christmas present for them, nicer than anything he had ever given them before. It was something that could n't be sent to them, so he wanted them to go all the way on the cars to his new home, to see it. Then after they had guessed everything they could think of, and were fairly hopping up and down with impatient curiosity, she 'd tell them what it was: *a new mother!*

She decided not to tell them that they were never coming back to the Junction to live. It would be better for them to think

MISS SANTA CLAUS

of this return to their father as just a visit until they were used to their new surroundings. It would make it easier for all concerned if they could be started off happy and pleasantly expectant. Then if Molly had grown up to be as nice a woman as she had been a young girl, she could safely trust the rest to her. The children would soon be loving her so much that they would n't want to come back.

But Mrs. Neal had not taken into account that her news was no longer a secret. Told to one or two friends in confidence, it had passed from lip to lip and had been discussed in so many homes, that half the children at the Junction knew that poor little Libby and Will'm Branfield were to have a stepmother, before they knew it themselves. Maudie Peters told Libby on their way home from school one day, and told it in such a tone that she made Libby feel that having a stepmother was about the worst calamity that could befall one. Libby denied it stoutly.

OF THE PULLMAN

"But you *are!*" Maudie insisted. "I heard mama and Aunt Louisa talking about it. They said they certainly felt sorry for you, and mama said that she hoped and prayed that *her* children would be spared such a fate, because stepmothers are always unkind."

Libby flew home with her tearful question, positive that Grandma Neal would say that Maudie was mistaken, but with a scared, shaky feeling in her knees, because Maudie had been so calmly and provokingly sure. Grandma Neal could deny only a part of Maudie's story.

"I'd like to spank that meddlesome Peters child!" she exclaimed indignantly. "Here I've been keeping it as a grand surprise for you that your father is going to give you a new mother for Christmas, and thinking what a fine time you'd have going on the cars to see them, and now Maudie has to go and tattle, and tell it in such an ugly way that she makes it seem like something bad, instead of the nicest thing that could happen to you. Listen, Libby!"

For Libby, at this confirmation of Maudie's tale, instead of the denial which she hoped for, had crooked her arm over her face, and was crying out loud into her little brown gingham sleeve, as if her heart would break. Mrs. Neal sat down and drew the sobbing child into her lap.

"Listen, Libby!" she said again. "This lady that your father has married, used to live here at the Junction when she was a little girl no bigger than you. Her name was Molly Blair, and she looked something like you—had the same color hair, and wore it in two little plaits just as you do. Everybody liked her. She was so gentle and kind she would n't have done anything to hurt any one's feelings any more than a little white kitten would. Your father was a boy then, and he lived here, and they went to school together and played together just as you and Walter Gray do. He's known her all her life, and he knew very well when

OF THE PULLMAN

he asked her to take the place of a mother to his little children that she'd be dear and good to you. Do you think that *you* could change so in growing up that you could be unkind to any little child that was put in your care?"

"No—o!" sobbed Libby.

"And neither could she!" was the emphatic answer. "You can just tell Maudie Peters that she doesn't know what she is talking about."

Libby repeated the message next day, emphatically and defiantly, with her chin in the air. That talk with Grandma Neal and another longer one which followed at bedtime, helped her to see things in their right light. Besides, several things which Grandma Neal told her made a visit to her father seem quite desirable. It would be fine to be in a city where there is something interesting to see every minute. She knew from other sources that in a city you might expect a hand-organ and a monkey to come down the street almost any day. And it

MISS SANTA CLAUS

would be grand to live in a house like the one they were going to, with an up-stairs to it, and a piano in the parlor.

But despite Mrs. Neal's efforts to set matters straight, the poison of Maudie's suggestion had done its work. Will'm had been in the room when Libby came home with her question, and the wild way she broke out crying made him feel that something awful was going to happen to them. He had never heard of a stepmother before. By some queer association of words his baby brain confused it with a step-ladder. There was such a ladder in the shop with a broken hinge. He was always being warned not to climb up on it. It might fall over with him and hurt him dreadfully. Even when everything had been explained to him, and he agreed that it would be lovely to take that long ride on the Pullman to see poor father, who was so lonely without his little boy, the poison of Maudie's suggestion still stayed with him. Something, he did n't know exactly what, but *something* was go-

OF THE PULLMAN

ing to fall with him and hurt him dreadfully if he did n't look out.

It's strange how much there is to learn about persons after you once begin to hear of them. It had been that way about Santa Claus. They had scarcely known his name, and then all of a sudden they heard so much, that instead of being a complete stranger he was a part of everything they said and did and thought. Now they were learning just as fast about stepmothers. Grandma and Uncle Neal and Miss Sally told them a great deal; all good things. And it was surprising how much else they had learned that was n't good, just by the wag of somebody's head, or a shrug of the shoulders or the pitying way some of the customers spoke to them.

When Libby came crying home from school the second time, because one of the boys called her Cinderella, and told her she would have to sit in the ashes and wear rags, and another one said no, she 'd be like Snowwhite, and have to eat poisoned apple,

MISS SANTA CLAUS

Grandma Neal was so indignant that she sent after Libby's books, saying that she would not be back at school any more.

Next day, Libby told Will'm the rest of what the boys had said to her. "All the stepmothers in stories are cruel like Cinderella's and Snow-white's, and sometimes they *are* cruel. They are always cruel when they have a tusk." Susie Peters told her what a tusk is, and showed her a picture of a cruel hag that had one. "It's an awful long ugly tooth that sticks away out of the side of your mouth like a pig's."

It was a puzzle for both Libby and Will'm to know whom to believe. They had sided with Maudie and the others in their faith in Santa Claus. How could they tell but that Grandma and Uncle Neal might be mistaken about their belief in stepmothers too?

Fortunately there were not many days in which to worry over the problem, and the few that lay between the time of Libby's leaving school and their going away, were filled with preparations for the journey.

OF THE PULLMAN

Of course Libby and Will'm had little part in that, except to collect the few toys they owned, and lay them beside the trunk which had been brought down from the attic to the sitting-room.

Libby had a grand washing of doll clothes one morning, and while she was hanging out the tiny garments on a string, stretched from one chair-back to another, Will'm proceeded to give his old Teddy Bear a bath in the suds which she had left in the basin. Plush does not take kindly to soap-suds, no matter how much it needs it. It would have been far better for poor Teddy to have started on his travels dirty, than to have become the pitiable, bedraggled-looking object that Libby snatched from the basin some time later, where Will'm put him to soak. It seemed as if the soggy cotton body never would dry sufficiently to be packed in the trunk, and Will'm would not hear to its being left behind, although it looked so dreadful that he did n't like to touch it. So it hung by a cord around its

MISS SANTA CLAUS

neck in front of the fire for two whole days, and everybody who passed it gave the cord a twist, so that it was kept turning like a roast on a spit.

There were more errands than usual to keep the children busy, and more ways in which they could help. As Christmas drew nearer and nearer somebody was needed in the shop every minute, and Mrs. Neal had her hands full with the extra work of looking over their clothes and putting every garment in order. Besides there was all the holiday baking to fill the shelves in the shop as well as in her own pantry.

So the children were called upon to set the table and help wipe the dishes. They dusted the furniture within their reach and fed the cat. They brought in chips from the woodhouse and shelled corn by the basketful for the old gray hens. And every day they carried the eggs very slowly and carefully from the nests to the pantry and put them one by one into the box of bran on the shelf. Then several mornings, all

OF THE PULLMAN

specially scrubbed and clean-aproned for the performance, they knelt on chairs by the kitchen table, and cut out rows and rows of little Christmas cakes, from the sheets of smoothly rolled dough on the floury cake boards. There were hearts and stars and cats and birds and all sorts of queer animals. Then after the baking there were delightful times when they hung breathlessly over the table, watching while scallops of pink or white icing were zigzagged around the stars and hearts, and pink eyes were put on the beasts and birds. Then of course the bowls which held the candied icing always had to be scraped clean by busy little fingers that went from bowl to mouth and back again, almost as fast as a kitten could lap with its pink tongue.

Oh, those last days in the old kitchen and sitting-room behind the shop were the best days of all, and it was good that Will'm and Libby were kept so busy every minute that they had no time to realize that they *were* last days, and that they were rapidly coming to an end. It was not until the last night that Will'm seemed to comprehend that they were really going away the next day.

He had been very busy helping get supper, for it was the kind that he specially liked. Uncle Neal had brought in a rabbit all ready skinned and dressed, which he had trapped that afternoon, and Will'm had gone around the room for nearly an hour, sniffing hungrily while it sputtered and browned in the skillet, smelling more tempting and delectable every minute. And he had watched while Grandma Neal lifted each crisp, brown piece up on a fork, and laid it on the hot waiting platter, and then stirred into the skillet the things that go to the making of a delicious cream gravy.

Suddenly in the ecstasy of anticipation Will'm was moved to throw his arms around Grandma Neal's skirts, gathering them in about her knees in such a violent hug that he almost upset her.

"Oh, rabbit *dravy!*" he exclaimed in a tone

"Oh, rabbit *dravy!*" he cried

OF THE PULLMAN

of such rapture that everybody laughed. Uncle Neal, who had already taken his place at the table, and was waiting too, with his chair tipped back on its hind legs, reached forward and gave Will'm's cheek a playful pinch.

"It's easy to tell what *you* think is the best tasting thing in the world," he said teasingly. "Just the smell of it puts the smile on your face that won't wear off."

Always when his favorite dish was on the table, Will'm passed his plate back several times for more. To-night after the fourth ladleful Uncle Neal hesitated. "Haven't you had about all that's good for you, kiddo?" he asked. "Remember you're going away in the morning, and you don't want to make yourself sick when you're starting off with just Libby to look after you."

There was no answer for a second. Then Will'm couldn't climb out of his chair fast enough to hide the trembling of his mouth and the gathering of unmanly tears. He

MISS SANTA CLAUS

cast himself across Mrs. Neal's lap, screaming, "I are n't going away! I won't leave my Dranma, and I won't go where there 'll never be any more good rabbit dravy!"

They quieted him after awhile, and comforted him with promises of the time when he should come back and be their little boy again, but he did not romp around as usual when he started to bed. He realized that when he came again maybe the little cribbed would be too small to hold him, and things would never be the same again.

Libby was quiet and inwardly tearful for another reason. They were to leave the very day on the night of which people hung up their stockings. Would Santa Claus know of their going and follow them? Will'm would be getting what he asked for, a ride on the Pullman, but how was she to get her gold ring? She lay awake quite a long while, worrying about it, but finally decided that she had been so good, so very good, that Santa would find some way to keep his part of the bargain. She had n't

OF THE PULLMAN

even fussed and rebelled about going back to her father as Maudie had advised her to do, and she had helped to persuade Will'm to accept quietly what could n't be helped.

The bell over the shop door went ting-a-ling many times that evening to admit belated customers, and as she grew drowsier and drowsier it began to sound like those other bells which would go tinkling along the Sky Road to-morrow night. Ah, that Sky Road! She would n't worry, remembering that the Christmas Angels came along that shining highway too. Maybe her heart's desire would be brought to her by one of them!

CHAPTER IV

ALTHOUGH L stands equally for Libby and Lion, and W for William and Whale, it is not to be inferred that the two small travelers thus labeled felt in any degree the courage of the king of beasts or the importance of the king of fishes. With every turn of the car wheels after they left the Junction, Will'm seemed to grow smaller and more bewildered, and Libby more frightened and forlorn. In Will'm's picture of this ride they had borne only their initials. Now they were faring forth tagged with their full names and their father's address. Miss Sally had done that "in case anything should happen."

If Miss Sally had not suggested that something might happen, Libby might not have had her fears aroused, and if they had been allowed to travel all the way in the

MISS SANTA CLAUS

toilet-room which Miss Sally and Grandma Neal showed them while the train waited its usual ten minutes at the Junction, they could have kept themselves too busy to think about the perils of pilgrimage. Never before had they seen water spurt from shining faucets into big white basins with chained-up holes at the bottom. It suggested magic to Libby, and she thought of several games they could have made, if they had not been hurried back to their seats in the car, and told that they must wait until time to eat, before washing their hands.

"I thought best to tell them that," said Miss Sally, as she and Mrs. Neal went slowly back to the shop. "Or Libby might have had most of the skin scrubbed off her and Will'm before night. And I know he'd drink the water cooler dry just for the pleasure of turning it into his new drinking cup you gave him, if he hadn't been told not to. Well, they're off, and so interested in everything that I don't believe they realized they were starting. There wasn't

MISS SANTA CLAUS

time for them to think that they were really leaving you."

"There'll be time enough before they get there," was the grim answer. "I should n't wonder if they both get to crying."

Then for fear that she should start to doing that same thing herself, she left Miss Sally to attend to the shop, and went briskly to work, putting the kitchen to rights. She had left the breakfast dishes until after the children's departure, for she had much to do for them, besides putting up two lunches. They left at ten o'clock, and could not reach their journey's end before half past eight that night. So both dinner and supper were packed in the big pasteboard box which had been stowed away under the seat with their suitcase.

Miss Sally was right about one thing. Neither child realized at first that the parting was final, until the little shop was left far behind. The novelty of their surroundings and their satisfaction at being really on board one of the wonderful cars which they

OF THE PULLMAN

had watched daily from the sitting-room window, made them feel that their best "S'posen" game had come true at last. But they had n't gone five miles until the landscape began to look unfamiliar. They had never been in this direction before, toward the hill country. Their drives behind Uncle Neal's old gray mare had always been the other way. Five miles more and they were strangers in a strange land. Fifteen miles, and they were experiencing the bitterness of "exiles from home" whom "splendor dazzles in vain." There was no charm left in the luxurious Pullman with its gorgeous red plush seats and shining mirrors. All the people they could see over the backs of those seats or reflected in those mirrors were strangers.

It made them even more lonely and aloof because the people did not seem to be strangers to each other. All up and down the car they talked and joked as people in this free and happy land always do when it's the day before Christmas and they are

MISS SANTA CLAUS

going home, whether they know each other or not. To make matters worse some of these strangers acted as if they knew Will'm and Libby, and asked them questions or snapped their fingers at them in passing in a friendly way. It frightened Libby, who had been instructed in the ways of travel, and she only drew closer to Will'm and said nothing when these strange faces smiled on her.

Presently Will'm gave a little muffled sob and Libby put her arm around his neck. It gave him a sense of protection, but it also started the tears which he had been fighting back for several minutes, and drawing himself up into a bunch of misery close beside her, he cried softly, his face hidden against her shoulder. If it had been a big capable shoulder, such as he was used to going to for comfort, the shower would have been over soon. But he felt its limitations. It was little and thin, only three years older and wiser than his own; as a support through unknown dangers not much to depend upon,

OF THE PULLMAN

still it was all he had to cling to, and he clung broken-heartedly and with scalding tears.

As for Libby she was realizing its limitations far more than he. His sobs shook her every time they shook him, and she could feel his tears, hot and wet on her arm through her sleeve. She started to cry herself, but fearing that if she did he might begin to roar so that they would be disgraced before everybody in the car, she bravely winked back her own tears and took an effective way to dry his.

Miss Sally had told them not to wash before it was time to eat, but of course Miss Sally had not known that Will'm was going to cry and smudge his face all over till it was a sight. If she could n't stop him somehow he 'd keep on till he was sick, and she 'd been told to take care of him. The little shoulder humped itself in a way that showed some motherly instinct was teaching it how to adjust itself to its new burden of responsibility, and she said in a comforting way,

MISS SANTA CLAUS

"Come on, brother, let's go and try what it's like to wash in that big white basin with the chained-up hole in the bottom of it."

There was a bowl apiece, and for the first five minutes their hands were white ducks swimming in a pond. Then the faucets were shining silver dragons, spouting out streams of water from their mouths to drown four little mermaids, who were not real mermaids, but children whom a wicked witch had changed to such and thrown into a pool. Then they blew soap-bubbles through their hands, till Will'm's squeal of delight over one especially fine bubble, which rested on the carpet a moment, instead of bursting, brought the porter to the door to see what was the matter.

They were not used to colored people. He pushed aside the red plush curtain and looked in, but the bubble had vanished, and all he saw was a slim little girl of seven snatching up a towel to polish the red cheeks of a chubby boy of four. When they went back to their seats their finger tips were curi-

He pushed aside the red plush curtain and looked in

OF THE PULLMAN

ously wrinkled from long immersion in the hot soap-suds, but the ache was gone out of their throats, and Libby thought it might be well for them to eat their dinner while their hands were so very clean. It was only quarter past eleven, but it seemed to them that they had been traveling nearly a whole day.

A chill of disappointment came to Will'm when his food was handed to him out of a pasteboard box. He had not thought to eat it in this primitive fashion. He had expected to sit at one of the little tables, but Libby did n't know what one had to do to gain the privilege of using them. The trip was not turning out to be all he had fondly imagined. Still the lunch in the pasteboard box was not to be despised. Even disappointment could not destroy the taste of Grandma Neal's chicken sandwiches and blackberry jam.

By the time they had eaten all they wanted, and tied up the box and washed their hands again (no bubbles and games this time for fear of the porter) it had begun to snow, and they found entertainment in watching the flakes that swirled against the panes in all sorts of beautiful patterns. They knelt on opposite seats, each against a window. Sometimes the snow seemed to come in sheets, shutting out all view of the little hamlets and farm houses past which they whizzed, with deep warning whistles, and sometimes it lifted to give them glimpses of windows with holly wreaths hanging from scarlet bows, and eager little faces peering out at the passing train—the way theirs used to peer, years ago, it seemed, before they started on this endless journey.

It makes one sleepy to watch the snow fall for a long time. After awhile Will'm climbed down from the window and cuddled up beside Libby again, with his soft bobbed hair tickling her ear, as he rested against her. He went to sleep so, and she put her arm around his neck again to keep him from slipping. The card with which Miss Sally had tagged him, slid along its cord and stuck

OF THE PULLMAN

up above his collar, prodding his chin. Libby pushed it back out of sight and felt under her dress for her own. They must be kept safely, "in case something should happen." She wondered what Miss Sally meant by that. What could happen? Their own Mr. Smiley was on the engine, and the conductor had been asked to keep an eye on them.

Then her suddenly awakened fear began to suggest answers. Maybe something might keep her father from coming to meet them. She and Will'm would n't know what to do or where to go. They 'd be lost in a great city like the little Match Girl was on Christmas eve, and they 'd freeze to death on some stranger's doorstep. There was a picture of the Match Girl thus frozen, in the Hans Andersen book which Susie Peters kept in her desk at school. There was a cruel stepmother picture in the same book, Libby remembered, and recollections of that turned her thoughts into still deeper channels of foreboding. What would *she* be

MISS SANTA CLAUS

like? What was going to happen to her and Will'm at the end of this journey if it ever came to an end? If only they could be back at the Junction, safe and sound—

The tears began to drip slowly. She wiped them away with the back of the hand that was farthest away from Will'm. She was miserable enough to die, but she did n't want him to wake up and find it out. A lady who had been watching her for some time, came and sat down in the opposite seat and asked her what was the matter, and if she was crying because she was homesick, and what was her name and how far they were going. But Libby never answered a single question. The tears just kept dripping and her mouth working in a piteous attempt to swallow her sobs, and finally the lady saw that she was frightening her, and only making matters worse by trying to comfort her, so she went back to her seat.

When Will'm wakened after a while and sat up, leaving Libby's arm all stiff and prickly from being bent in one position so

OF THE PULLMAN

long, the train had been running for miles through a lonely country where nobody seemed to live. Just as he rubbed his eyes wide awake they came to a forest of Christmas trees. At least, they looked as if all they needed to make them that, was for some one to fasten candles on their snow-laden boughs. Then the whistle blew the signal that meant that the train was about to stop, and Will'm scrambled up on his knees again, and they both looked out expectantly.

There was no station at this place of stopping. Only by special order from some high official did this train come to a halt here, so somebody of importance must be coming aboard. All they saw at first was a snowy road opening through the grove of Christmas trees, but standing in this road, a few rods from the train, was a sleigh drawn by two big black horses. They had bells on their bridles which went ting-a-ling whenever they shook their heads or pawed the snow. The children could not see a trunk being put into the baggage car farther up

MISS SANTA CLAUS

the track, but they saw what happened in the delay.

A half-grown boy, a suitcase in one hand and a pile of packages in his arms, dashed towards the car, leaving a furry old gentleman in the sleigh to hold the horses. The old gentleman's coat was fur, and his cap was fur, and so was the great rug which covered him. Under the fur cap was thick white hair, and all over the bottom of his face was a bushy white beard. And his cheeks were red and his eyes were laughing, and if he was n't Santa Claus's own self he certainly looked enough like the nicest pictures of him to be his own brother.

On the seat beside him was a young girl, who, waiting only long enough to plant a kiss on one of those rosy cheeks above the snowy beard, sprang out of the sleigh and ran after the boy as hard as she could go. She was not more than sixteen, but she looked like a full-grown young lady to Libby, for her hair was tucked up under her little fur cap

And ran after the boy as hard as she could go

OF THE PULLMAN

with its scarlet quill, and the long, fur-bordered red coat she wore, reached her ankles. One hand was thrust through a row of holly wreaths, and she was carrying all the bundles both arms could hold.

By the time the boy had deposited his load in the section opposite the children's, and dashed back down the aisle, there was a call of "All aboard!" They met at the door, he and the pretty girl, she laughing and nodding her thanks over her pile of bundles. He raised his hat and bolted past, but stopped an instant, just before jumping off the train, to run back and thrust his head in the door and call out laughingly, "Good-by, Miss Santa Claus!"

Everybody in the car looked up and smiled, and turned and looked again as she went up the aisle, for a lovelier Christmas picture could not be imagined than the one she made in her long red coat, her arms full of packages and wreaths of holly. The little fur cap with its scarlet feather was powdered with snow, and the frosty wind had

MISS SANTA CLAUS

brought such a glow to her cheeks and a sparkle in her eyes that she looked the living embodiment of Christmas cheer. Her entrance seemed to bring with it the sense of all holiday joy, just as the cardinal's first note holds in it the sweetness of a whole spring.

Will'm edged along the seat until he was close beside Libby, and the two sat and stared at her with wide-eyed interest.

That boy had called her Miss Santa Claus!

If the sleigh which brought her had been drawn by reindeer, and she had carried her pack on her back instead of in her arms, they could not have been more spellbound. They scarcely breathed for a few moments. The radiant, glowing creature took off the long red coat and gave it to the porter to hang up, then she sat down and began sorting her packages into three piles. It took some time to do this, as she had to refer constantly to a list of names on a long strip of paper, and compare them with the names on

OF THE PULLMAN

the bundles. While she was doing this the conductor came for her ticket and she asked several questions.

Yes, he assured her, they were due at Eastbrook in fifteen minutes and would stop there long enough to take water.

"Then I'll have plenty of time to step off with these things," she said. "And I'm to leave some at Centreville and some at Ridgely."

When the conductor said something about helping Santa Claus, she answered laughingly, "Yes, Uncle thought it would be better for me to bring these breakable things instead of trusting them to the chimney route." Then in answer to a question which Libby did not hear, "Oh, that will be all right. Uncle telephoned all down the line and arranged to have some one meet me at each place."

When the train stopped at Eastbrook, both the porter and conductor came to help her gather up her first pile of parcels, and people in the car stood up and craned their necks

MISS SANTA CLAUS

to see what she did with them. Libby and Will'm could see. They were on the side next to the station. She gave them to several people who seemed to be waiting for her. Almost immediately she was surrounded by a crowd of young men and girls, all shaking hands with her and talking at once. From the remarks which floated in through the open vestibule, it seemed that they all must have been at some party with her the night before. A chorus of good-byes and Merry Christmases followed her into the car when she had to leave them and hurry aboard. This time she came in empty handed, and this time people looked up and smiled openly into her face, and she smiled back as if they were all friends, sharing their good times together.

At Centreville she darted out with the second lot. Farther down a number of people were leaving the day coaches, but no one was getting off the Pullman. She did not leave the steps, but leaned over and called to an old colored-man who stood with

OF THE PULLMAN

a market basket on his arm. "This way, Mose. Quick!"

Then Will'm and Libby heard her say: "Tell 'Old Miss' that Uncle Norse sent this holly. He wanted her to have it because it grew on his own place and is the finest in the country. Don't knock the berries off, and do be careful of this biggest bundle. I wouldn't have it broken for anything. And—oh, yes, Mose" (this in a lower tone), "this is for you."

What it was that passed from the little white hand into the worn brown one of the old servitor was not discovered by the interested audience inside the car, but they heard a chuckle so full of pleasure that some of them echoed it unconsciously.

"Lawd bless you, li'l' Miss, you sho' is the flowah of the Santa Claus fambly!"

When she came in this time, a motherly old lady near the door stopped her, and smiling up at her through friendly spectacles, asked if she were going home for Christmas.

"Yes!" was the enthusiastic answer.

MISS SANTA CLAUS

"And you know what that means to a Freshman—her first homecoming after her first term away at school. I should have been there four days ago. Our vacation began last Friday, but I stopped over for a houseparty at my cousin's. I was wild to get home, but I could n't miss this visit, for she 's my dearest chum as well as my cousin, and last night was her birthday. Maybe you noticed all those people who met me at Eastbrook. They were at the party."

"That was nice," answered the little old lady, bobbing her head. "Very nice, my dear. And now you 'll be getting home at the most beautiful time in all the year."

"Yes, *I* think so," was the happy answer. "Christmas eve to me always means going around with father to take presents, and I would n't miss it for anything in the world. I 'm glad there 's enough snow this year for us to use the sleigh. We had to take the auto last year, and it was n't half as much fun."

Libby and Will'm scarcely moved after

OF THE PULLMAN

that, all the way to Ridgely. Nor did they take their eyes off her. Mile after mile they rode, barely batting an eyelash, staring at her with unabated interest. At Ridgley she handed off all the rest of the packages and all of the holly wreaths but two. These she hung up out of the way over her windows, then taking out a magazine, settled herself comfortably in the end of the seat to read.

On her last trip up the aisle she had noticed the wistful, unsmiling faces of her little neighbors across the way, and she wondered why it was that the only children in the coach should be the only ones who seemed to have no share in the general joyousness. Something was wrong, she felt sure, and while she was cutting the leaves of the magazine, she stole several glances in their direction. The little girl had an anxious pucker of the brows sadly out of place in a face that had not yet outgrown its baby innocence of expression. She looked so little and lorn and troubled about something, that Miss Santa Claus made up her mind to comfort her as soon as she had an opportunity. She knew better than to ask for her confidence as the well-meaning lady had done earlier in the day.

When she began to read, Will'm drew a long breath and stretched himself. There was no use watching now when it was evident that she was n't going to do anything for awhile, and sitting still so long had made him fidgety. He squirmed off the seat, and up into the next one, unintentionally wiping his feet on Libby's dress as he did so. It brought a sharp reproof from the overwrought Libby, and he answered back in the same spirit.

Neither was conscious that their voices could be heard across the aisle above the noise of the train. The little fur cap with the scarlet feather bent over the magazine without the slightest change in posture, but there was no more turning of pages. The piping, childish voices were revealing a far more interesting story than the printed one the girl was scanning. She heard her own

OF THE PULLMAN

name mentioned. They were disputing about her.

Too restless to sit still, and with no way in which to give vent to his all-consuming energy, Will'm was ripe for a squabble. It came very soon, and out of many allusions to past and present, and dire threats as to what might happen to him at the end of the journey if he did n't mend his ways, the interested listener gathered the principal facts in their history. The fuss ended in a shower of tears on Will'm's part, and the consequent smudging of his face with his grimy little hands which wiped them away, so that he had to be escorted once more behind the curtain to the shining faucets and the basin with the chained-up hole at the bottom.

When they came back Miss Santa Claus had put away her magazine and taken out some fancy work. All she seemed to be doing was winding some red yarn over a pencil, around and around and around. But presently she stopped and tied two ends with

MISS SANTA CLAUS

a jerk, and went snip, snip with her scissors, and there in her fingers was a soft fuzzy ball. When she had snipped some more, and trimmed it all over, smooth and even, it looked like a little red cherry. In almost no time she had two wool cherries lying in her lap. She was just beginning the third when the big ball of yarn slipped out of her fingers, and rolled across the aisle right under Libby's feet. She sprang to pick it up and take it back.

"Thank you, dear," was all that Miss Santa Claus said, but such a smile went with it, that Libby, smoothing her skirts over her knees as she primly took her seat again, felt happier than she had since leaving the Junction. It wasn't two minutes till the ball slipped and rolled away again. This time Will'm picked it up, and she thanked him in the same way. But very soon when both scissors and ball spilled out of her lap and Libby politely brought her one and Will'm the other, she did not take them.

"I wonder," she said, "if you children

OF THE PULLMAN

could n't climb up here on the seat with me and hold this old Jack and Jill of a ball and scissors. Every time one falls down and almost breaks its crown, the other goes tumbling after. I 'm in such a hurry to get through. Could n't you stay and help me a few minutes?"

"Yes, ma'am," said Libby, primly and timidly, sitting down on the edge of the opposite seat with the ball in her hands. Miss Santa Claus put an arm around Will'm and drew him up on the seat beside her. "There," she said. "You hold the scissors, Will'm, and when I 'm through winding the ball that Libby holds, I 'll ask you to cut the yarn for me. Did you ever see such scissors, Libby? They 're made in the shape of a witch. See! She sits upon the handles, and when the blades are closed they make the peak of her long pointed cap. They came from the old witch town of Salem."

Libby darted a half-frightened look at her. She had called them both by name! Had *she* been listening down the chimney,

MISS SANTA CLAUS

too? And those witch scissors! They looked as if they might be a charm to open all sorts of secrets. Maybe she knew some charm to keep stepmothers from being cruel. Oh, if she only dared to ask! Of course Libby knew that one must n't "pick up" with strangers and tell them things. Miss Sally had warned her against that. But this was different. Miss Santa Claus was *more* than just a person.

If Pan were to come piping out of the woods, who, with any music in him, would not respond with all his heart to the magic call? If Titania were to beckon with her gracious wand, who would not be drawn into her charmèd circle gladly? So it was these two little wayfarers heard the call and swayed to the summons of one who not only shed the influence, but shared the name of the wonderful Spirit of Yule.

CHAPTER V

WITH Libby to hold the ball and unwind the yarn as fast as it was needed, and Will'm to cut it with the witch scissors every time Miss Santa Claus said "snip!" it was not long before half a dozen little wool cherries lay in her lap. Then they helped twist the yarn into cords on which to tie the balls, and watched with eyes that never lost a movement of her deft fingers, while she fastened the cords to the front of a red crocheted jacket, which she took from her suitcase.

"There!" she exclaimed, holding it up for them to admire. "That is to go in the stocking of a poor little fellow no larger than Will'm. He's lame and has to stay in bed all the time, and he asked Santa Claus to bring him something soft and warm to put

MISS SANTA CLAUS

on when he is propped up in bed to look at his toys."

Out of a dry throat Libby at last brought up the question she had been trying to find courage for.

"Is Santa Claus your father?"

"No, but father and Uncle Norse are so much like him that people often get them all mixed up, just as they do twins, and since Uncle Santa has grown so busy, he gets father to attend to a great deal of his business. In fact our whole family has to help. He could n't possibly get around to everybody as he used to when the cities were smaller and fewer. Lately he has been leaving more and more of his work to us. He's even taken to adopting people into his family so that they can help him. In almost every city in the world now, he has an adopted brother or sister or relative of some sort, and sometimes children not much bigger than you, ask to be counted as members of his family. It's so much fun to help."

Libby pondered over this news a moment

OF THE PULLMAN

before she asked another question. "Then does he come to see them and tell them what to do?"

"No, indeed! Nobody ever *sees* him. He just sends messages, something like wireless telegrams. You know what they are?"

Libby shook her head. She had never heard of them. Miss Santa Claus explained. "And his messages pop into your head just that way," she added. "I was as busy as I could be one day, studying my Algebra lesson, when all of a sudden, pop came the thought into my head that little Jamie Fitch wanted a warm red jacket to wear when he sat up in bed, and that Uncle Santa wanted me to make it. I went down town that very afternoon and bought the wool, and I knew that I was not mistaken by the way I felt afterward, so glad and warm and Christmasy. That's why all his family love to help him. He gives them such a happy feeling while they are doing it."

It was Will'm's turn now for a question.

He asked it abruptly with a complete change of base.

"Did you ever see a stepmother?"

"Yes, indeed! And Cousin Rosalie has one. She's Uncle Norse's wife. I've just been visiting them."

"Has she got a tush?"

"A *what?*" was the astonished answer.

"He means tusk," explained Libby. "All the cruel ones have 'm, Susie Peters says."

"Sticking out this way, like a pig's," Will'm added eagerly, at the same time pulling his lip down at one side to show a little white tooth in the place where the dreadful fang would have grown, had he been the cruel creature in question.

"Mercy, *no!*" was the horrified exclamation. "That kind live only in fairy tales along with ogres and giants. Didn't you know that?"

Will'm shook his head. "Me an' Libby was afraid ours would be that way, and if she is we're going to do something to her.

OF THE PULLMAN

We're going to shut her up in a nawful dark cellar, or—or *something*."

Miss Santa looked grave. Here was a dreadful misunderstanding. Somebody had poisoned these baby minds with suspicions and doubts which might embitter their whole lives. If she had been only an ordinary fellow passenger she might not have felt it her duty to set them straight. But no descendant of the family of which she was a member, could come face to face with such a wrong, without the impulse to make it right. It was an impulse straight from the Sky Road. In the carol service in the chapel, the night before she left school, the dean had spoken so beautifully of the way they might all follow the Star, this Christmastide, with their gifts of frankincense and myrrh, even if they had no gold. Here was her opportunity, she thought, if she were only wise enough to say the right thing!

Before she could think of a way to begin, a waiter came through the car, sounding the first call for dinner. Time was flying.

MISS SANTA CLAUS

She'd have to hurry, and make the most of it before the journey came to an end. Putting the little crocheted jacket back into her suitcase and snapping the clasps she stood up.

"Come on," she said, holding out a hand to each. "We'll go into the dining-car and get something to eat."

Libby thought of the generous supper in the pasteboard box which they had been told to eat as soon as it was dark, but she allowed herself to be led down the aisle without a word. A higher power was in authority now. She was as one drawn into a fairy ring.

Now at last, the ride on the Pullman blossomed into all that Will'm had pictured it to be. There was the gleam of glass, the shine of silver, the glow of shaded candles, and himself at one of the little tables, while the train went flying through the night like a mighty winged dragon, breathing smoke and fire as it flew.

Miss Santa Claus studied the printed card

OF THE PULLMAN

beside her plate a moment, and then looked into her pocketbook before she wrote the order. She smiled a little while she was writing it. She wanted to make this meal one that they would always remember, and was sure that children who lived at such a place as the Junction had never before eaten strawberries on Christmas eve; a snow-covered Christmas eve at that. She had been afraid for just a moment, when she first peeped into her purse, that there was n't enough left for her to get them.

No one had anything to say while the order was being filled. Will'm and Libby were too busy looking at the people and things around them, and their companion was too busy thinking about something she wanted to tell them after awhile. Presently the steward passed their table, and Will'm gave a little start of recognition, but he said nothing. It was the same man whose locket he had found, and who had promised to tell Santa Claus about him. Evidently he had told, for here was Will'm in full enjoyment

MISS SANTA CLAUS

of what he had longed for. The man did not look at Will'm, however. He was too busy attending to the wants of impatient grown people to notice a quiet little boy who sat next the wall and made no demands.

Then the waiter came, balancing an enormous tray on one hand, high above his head, and the children watched him with the breathless fascination with which they would have watched a juggler play his tricks. It was a simple supper, for Miss Santa Claus was still young enough to remember what had been served to her in her nursery days, but it was crowned by a dish of enormous strawberries, such as Will'm had seen in the refrigerator of the car kitchen, but nowhere else. They never grew that royal size at the Junction.

But what made the meal more than one of mortal enjoyment, and transformed the earthly food into ambrosia of the gods, was that while they sifted the powdered sugar over their berries, Miss Santa Claus began to tell them a story. It was about the Princess

It was about the Princess Ina

OF THE PULLMAN

Ina, who had six brothers whom a wicked witch changed into swans. It was a very interesting story, the way she told it, and more than once both Libby and Will'm paused with their spoons half way from berries to mouth, the better to listen. It was quite sad, too, for only once in twenty-four hours, and then just for a few moments, could the princes shed their swan-skins and be real brothers again. At these times they would fly back to their sister Ina, and with tears in their eyes, beg her to help them break the cruel charm.

At last she found a way, but it would be a hard way for her. She must go alone, and in the fearsome murk of the gloaming, to a spot where wild asters grow. The other name for them is star-flower. If she could pick enough of these star-flowers to weave into a mantle for each brother, which would cover him from wing-tip to wing-tip, then they would be free from the spell as soon as it was thrown over them. But the flowers must be gathered in silence. A single word

MISS SANTA CLAUS

spoken aloud would undo all her work. And it would be a hard task, for the starflowers grew only among briars and weeds, and her hands would be scratched with thorns and stung by nettles. Yet no matter how badly she was torn or blistered she must not break her silence by one word of complaint.

Now the way Miss Santa told that story made you feel that it was *you* and not the Princess Ina who was groping through the fearsome gloaming after the magic flowers. Once Libby felt the scratch of the thorns so plainly that she said "oo-oh" in a whisper, and looked down at her own hands, half expecting to see blood on them. And Will'm forgot to eat entirely, when it came to the time of weaving the last mantle, and there wasn't quite enough material to piece it out to the last wing-tip. Still there was enough to change the last swan back into a real brother again, even if one arm never was quite as it should be; and when all six brothers stood around their dear sister,

OF THE PULLMAN

weeping tears of joy at their deliverance, Will'm's face shone as if he had just been delivered from the same fate himself.

"Now," said Miss Santa Claus, when the waiter had brought the bill and gone back for some change, "you must never, never forget that story as long as you live. I've told it to you because it's a true charm that can be used for many things. Aunt Ruth told it to me. She used it long ago, when she wanted to change Rosalie into a real daughter, and I used it once when I wanted to change a girl who was just a pretend friend, into a real one. *And you are to use it to change your stepmother into a real mother!* I'll tell you how when we go back to our seats."

On the way back they stopped in the vestibule between the cars for a breath of fresh air, and to look out on the snow-covered country, lying white in the moonlight. The flakes were no longer falling.

"I see the Sky Road!" sang out Will'm in a happy sort of chant, pointing up at the glittering milky way. "Pretty soon the drate big reindeer 'll come running down that road!"

"And the Christmas Angels," added Libby reverently, in a half whisper.

"And there's where the star-flowers grow," Miss Santa Claus chimed in, as if she were singing. "Once there was a dear poet who called the stars 'the forget-me-nots of the angels.' I believe I'll tell you about them right now, while we're out here where we can look up at them. Oh, I wonder if I can make it plain enough for you to understand me!"

With an arm around each child's shoulder to steady them while they stood there, rocking and swaying with the motion of the lurching train, she began:

"It's this way. When you go home, probably there'll be lots of things that you won't like, and that you won't want to do. Things that will seem as disagreeable as Ina's task was to her. They won't scratch and blister your hands, but they'll make you

OF THE PULLMAN

feel all scratchy and hot and cross. But if you go ahead as Ina did, without opening your lips to complain, *it will be like picking a little white star-flower whose name is obedience.* The more you pick of them the more you will have to weave into your mantle. And sometimes you will see a chance to do something to help her or to please her, without waiting to be asked. You may have to stop playing to do it, and give up your own pleasure. That will scratch your feelings some, *but doing it will be like picking a big golden star-flower whose name is kindness.* And if you keep on doing this, day after day as Ina did, with never a word of complaint, the time will come when you have woven a big, beautiful mantle whose name is love. And when it is big enough to reach from 'wing-tip to wing-tip' you'll find that she has grown to be just like a real mother. Do you understand?"

"Yes, ma'am," answered Libby solemnly. Will'm did not answer, but the far-off look

MISS SANTA CLAUS

in his eyes showed that he was pondering over what she had just told him.

"Now we must run along in," she said briskly. "It's cold out here." Inside, she looked at her watch. It was after seven. Only a little more than an hour, and the children would be at the end of their journey. Not much longer than that and she would reach hers. It had been a tiresome day for both Libby and Will'm. Although their eyes shone with the excitement of it, the Sandman was not far away. It was their regular bedtime, and they were yawning. At a word from Miss Santa Claus the porter brought pillows and blankets. She made up a bed for each on opposite seats and tucked them snugly in.

"Now," she said, bending over them, "You'll have time for a nice long nap before your father comes to take you off. But before you go to sleep, I want to tell you one more thing that you must remember forever. *You must always get the right kind of start*. It's like hooking

OF THE PULLMAN

up a dress, you know. If you start crooked it will keep on being crooked all the way down to the bottom, unless you undo it and begin over. So if I were you, I'd begin to work that star-flower charm the first thing in the morning. Remember you can work it on anybody if you try hard enough. And remember that it is *true,* just as true as it is that you're each going to have a Christmas stocking!"

She stooped over each in turn and kissed their eyelids down with a soft touch of her smiling lips that made Libby thrill for days afterward, whenever she thought of it. It seemed as if some royal spell had been laid upon them with those kisses; some spell to close their eyes to nettles and briars, and help them to see only the star-flowers.

In less than five minutes both Libby and Will'm were sound asleep, and the porter was carrying the holly wreaths and the red coat and the suitcase back to the state-room which had been vacated at the last stopping place. In two minutes more Miss Santa

MISS SANTA CLAUS

Claus had emptied her suitcase out on the seat beside her, and was scrabbling over the contents in wild haste. For no sooner had she mentioned stockings to the children than pop had come one of those messages straight from the Sky Road, which could not be disregarded. Knowing that she would be on the train with the two children from the Junction, Santa Claus was leaving it to her to provide stockings for them.

It worried her at first, for she could n't see her way clear to doing it on such short notice and in such limited quarters. But she had never failed him since he had first allowed her the pleasure of helping him, and she did n't intend to now. Her mind had to work as fast as her fingers. There was n't a single thing among her belongings that she could make stockings of, unless— she sighed as she picked it up and shook out the folds of the prettiest kimono she had ever owned. It was the softest possible shade of gray with white cherry blossoms scattered over it, and it was bordered in

OF THE PULLMAN

wide bands of satin the exact color of a shining ripe red cherry. There was nothing else for it, the lovely kimono must be shorn of its glory, at least on one side. Maybe she could split what was left on the other side, and reborder it all with narrower bands. But even if she couldn't, she must take it. The train was leaping on through the night. There was no time to spare.

Snip! Snip! went the witch scissors, and the long strip of cherry satin was loose in her hands. Twenty minutes later two bright red stockings lay on the seat in front of her, bordered with silver tinsel. She had run the seams hastily with white thread, all she had with her, but the stitches did not show, being on the inside. Even if they had pulled themselves into view in places, all defects in sewing were hidden by the tinsel with which the stockings were bordered. She had unwound it from a wand which she was carrying home with several other favors from the german of the night before. The wand was so long that it went into her suitcase only by laying it in diagonally. It had been wrapped around and around with yards of tinsel, tipped with a silver-gauze butterfly.

While she stitched she tried to think of something to put into the stockings. Her only hope was in the trainboy, and she sent the porter to bring him. But when he came he had little to offer. As it was Christmas eve everybody had wanted his wares and he was nearly sold out. Not a nut, not an apple, not even a package of chewing gum could he produce. But he did have somewhere among his things, he said, two little toy lanterns, with red glass sides, filled with small mixed candies, and he had several oranges left. Earlier in the day he had had small glass pistols filled with candy. He departed to get the stock still on hand.

When the lanterns proved to be miniature conductor's lanterns Miss Santa Claus could have clapped her hands with satisfaction. Children who played train so much would be delighted with them. She thrust

OF THE PULLMAN

one into each stocking with an orange on top. They just filled the legs, but there was a dismal limpness of foot which sadly betrayed its emptiness. With another glance at her watch Miss Santa Claus hurried back to the dining-car. The tables were nearly empty, and she found the steward by the door. She showed him the stockings and implored him to think of something to help fill them. Hadn't he nuts, raisins, *anything,* even little cakes, that she could get in a hurry?

He suggested salted almonds and after-dinner mints, and sent a waiter flying down the aisle to get some. While she waited she explained that they were for two children who had come by themselves all the way from the Junction. It was little Will'm's first ride on a Pullman. The words "Junction" and "Will'm" seemed to recall something to the steward.

"I wonder if it could be the same little chap who found my locket," he said. "I took his name intending to send him some-

MISS SANTA CLAUS

thing Christmas, but was so busy I never thought of it again."

The waiter was back with the nuts and mints. Miss Santa Claus paid for them, and hurriedly returned to the state-room. She had to search through her things again to find some tissue paper to wrap the salted almonds in. They'd spoil the red satin if put in without covering. While she was doing it the steward came to the door.

"I beg pardon, Miss," he said. "But would you mind showing me the little fellow? If it *is* the same one, I'd like to leave him a small trick I've got here."

She pointed down the aisle to the seat where Will'm lay sound asleep, one dimpled fist cuddled under his soft chin. After a moment's smiling survey the man came back.

"That's the kid all right," he told her. "And he seemed to be so powerful fond of anything that has to do with a train, I thought it would please him to find this in his stocking."

OF THE PULLMAN

He handed her a small-sized conductor's punch. "I use it to keep tally on the order cards," he explained, "but I won't need it on the rest of this run."

"How lovely!" exclaimed Miss Santa Claus. "I know he'll be delighted, and I'm much obliged to you myself, for helping me make his stocking fuller and nicer."

She opened the magazine after he had gone, and just to try the punch closed it down on one of the leaves. Clip, it went, and the next instant she uttered a soft little cry of pleasure. The clean-cut hole that the punch had made in the margin was star shaped, and on her lap, where it had fallen from the punch, was a tiny white paper star.

"Oh, it will help him to remember the charm!" she whispered, her eyes shining with the happy thought. "If I only had some kind of a reminder for Libby, too!"

Then, all of a sudden came another message, straight from the Sky Road! She could give Libby the little gold ring which

MISS SANTA CLAUS

had fallen to her lot the night before in her slice of the birthday cake. There had been a ring, a thimble and a dime in the cake, and she had drawn the ring. It was so small, just a child's size, that she could n't wear it, but she was taking it home to put in her memory book. It had been such a beautiful evening that she wanted to mark it with that little golden circlet, although of course it was n't possible for her to forget such a lovely time, even in centuries. And Libby *might* forget about the star-flowers unless she had a daily reminder.

She held it in her hand a moment, hesitating, till the message came again, *"Send it!"* Then there was no longer any indecision. When she shut it in its little box, and stuffed the box down past the lantern and the orange and the nuts and the peppermints into the very toe, such a warm, glad Christmasy feeling sent its glow through her, that she knew past all doubting she had interpreted the Sky Road message aright.

Many of the passengers had left the car

OF THE PULLMAN

by this time, and the greater number of those who remained were nodding uncomfortably in their seats. But those who happened to be awake and alert saw a picture they never forgot, when a lovely young girl, her face alight with the joy of Christmas love and giving, stole down the aisle and silently fastened something on the back of the seat above each little sleeper. It was a stocking, red and shining as a cherry, and silver-bordered with glistening fairy fringe.

When they looked again she had disappeared, but the stockings still hung there, tokens which were to prove to those same little sleepers on their awakening that the star-flower charm is true. For love indeed works miracles, and every message from the Sky Road is but an echo of the one the Christmas angels sang when first they came along that shining highway, the heralds of good-will and peace to all the earth.

CHAPTER VI

CHRISTMAS morning when Will'm awoke, he was as bewildered as if he had opened his eyes in a new world. He was in a little white bed, such as he had never seen before, and the blankets were blue, with a border of white bunnies around each one. Between him and the rest of the room was a folding screen, like a giant picture-book cover, showing everybody in Mother Goose's whole family. He lay staring at it awhile, and when he recognized Tommy Tucker and Simple Simon and Mother Hubbard's dog, he did n't feel quite so lost and strange as he did at first.

Always at the Junction he had to lie still until Uncle Neal made the fire and the room was warm; but here it was already warm, and he could hear steam hissing somewhere. It seemed to be coming from the gilt pipes

MISS SANTA CLAUS

under the window. Wondering what was on the other side of the screen, he slid out from under the bunny blankets and peeped cautiously around the wall of Mother Goose pictures. It was Libby on the other side in another little white bed just like his. With one spring he pounced up on top of it, and squirmed in beside her.

The first moment of Libby's awakening was as bewildering as Will'm's had been. Then she began to have a confused recollection of the night before. She remembered being lifted from the pillow on the car seat, and hugged and kissed, and having her limp, sleepy arms thrust into elusive coat sleeves. Somebody held her hand and hurried her down the aisle after her father, who was carrying Will'm, because he was so sound asleep that they could n't even put his overcoat on him. It was just wrapped around him. Then she remembered jolting across the city in an omnibus, with her head on a muff in a lady's lap, and of leaning against that same lady afterwards while her clothes

MISS SANTA CLAUS

were being unbuttoned, and her eyelids kept falling shut. She had never been so sleepy in her whole life, that she could remember.

Suddenly she sat straight up in bed and stared at something hanging on the post of the low footboard; a Christmas stocking all red and silver, and for her! Even from where she was she could read the name that Miss Santa Claus had printed in big letters on the scrap of paper pinned to it: "LIBBY."

Only those who have thrilled with that same speechless rapture can know a tithe of the bliss which filled Libby's soul, as she seized it, her first Christmas stocking, and began to explore it with fingers trembling in their eagerness. When down in the very toe she found the "little shiny gold ring like Maudie Peters's," all she had breath for was a long indrawn "Aw-aw-aw!" of ecstasy.

"Oh, Will'm!" she exclaimed, when she could find speech, "are n't you glad we bleeved?"

OF THE PULLMAN

"But I are n't got any stocking," he said gloomily, eyeing her enviously while she slipped the ring on her finger and waved her hand around to admire the effect.

"But you got all you asked for: the ride on the cars," she reminded him cheerfully. "Did you look on your post to see if there was anything?" No, he had not looked, and at the suggestion he sprang out of Libby's bed like a furry white kitten in his little teazledown nightdrawers made with feet to them, and knelt on top of his own bunny blankets.

"Oh, Libby! There *is* one. There *is!*" he cried excitedly. "It slipped around to the back of the post where I could n't see it before. There 's an orange and a lantern just like yours, and what 's this? Oh, *look!*"

The awesome joy of his voice made Libby join him on the other side of the Mother Goose screen, and she snatched the little punch from him almost as eagerly as he had snatched it from the stocking, to try it on

MISS SANTA CLAUS

the slip of paper which bore the name "WILL'M," pinned across the toe. They had watched the conductor using his the previous day, and had each wished for one to use in playing their favorite game. Clip, it went, and their heads bumped together in their eagerness to see the result. There in the paper was a clear-cut hole in the shape of a tiny star, and on the blanket where it had fallen from the hole, was the star itself. The punch which the conductor had used made round holes. This was a thousand times nicer.

Up till this moment, in the bewilderment of finding themselves in their new surroundings, the children had forgotten all about Miss Santa Claus and her story of Ina and the swans. But now Libby looked up, as Will'm snatched back the punch and began clipping holes in the paper as fast as he could clip. The shower of stars falling on the blanket made her think of the star-flower charm, which they had been advised to begin using first thing in the morning. Immedi-

The shower of stars falling on the blanket made her think
of the star-flower

OF THE PULLMAN

ately Libby retired to her side of the screen and began to dress.

"Don't you know," she reminded Will'm, "she said that we must be particular to start right. It's like hooking up a dress. If you start crooked, everything will keep on being crooked all the way down. I'm going to get started right, for I've found it's just as easy to be good as it is to be bad when you once get used to trying."

Will'm wasn't paying attention. He had punched the slip of paper so full of holes it wouldn't hold another one, and now he tried the punch on the edge of one of the soft blankets, just to see if it would make a blue star drop out. But the punch didn't cut blankets as evenly as it did paper. Only a snip of wool came loose and stuck in the punch, and the hole almost closed up afterward when he picked at it a little. He didn't show it to Libby.

That is the last he thought of the charm that day, for their father put his head in at the door to call "Merry Christmas," and say

MISS SANTA CLAUS

that he'd be in in a few minutes to help him into his clothes, and that their mother would come too to tie Libby's hair-ribbons and hurry things along, because they must hustle down to breakfast to see the grand surprise she had for them.

Then Will'm hurried so fast that he was in his clothes by the time his father came in; he had even washed his own face and hands after a fashion, and there was nothing to be done for him but to brush his hair, and while his father was doing that, he talked and joked in such an entertaining way that Will'm did not feel at all strange with him as he had expected to do. But he felt strange when presently his father exclaimed, *"Here's* mother," and somebody put her arms around him and kissed him and wished him a Merry Christmas, and then did the same to Libby.

She looked so smiling and home-like that she seemed more like Miss Sally Watts or somebody they had known at the Junction than a stepmother. If Will'm hadn't

OF THE PULLMAN.

known that she was one, and that he was expected to love her, he would have liked her right away, almost as much as he did Miss Sally. But he felt shy and uncomfortable, and he did n't know what to call her. The name "mama" did not belong to her. It never could. That belonged to the beautiful picture hanging on the wall where it could be seen from both little beds, last thing at night and first thing in the morning. They had had a smaller picture just like it at the Junction, but this was more beautiful because it showed the soft pink in her cheeks and the blue in her smiling eyes, and the other was only a photograph. Will'm knew as well as Libby did that the reason their father had kept talking about "your mother" all the time he was brushing his hair, was because he wanted them to call her that. But he *could n't!* He did n't know her well enough. He felt that it would choke him to call her anything but *She* or *Her*.

While his father carried him down to

breakfast pick-a-back, *She* led Libby by the hand, and told about finding the stockings pinned to the car seats, and about a beautiful girl who suddenly appeared beside her in the aisle, and asked her to be sure to hang them where the children could find them first thing in the morning. Santa Claus had asked her to be sure that they got them. She had on a long red coat and a little fur cap with a red feather in it. There was n't any time to ask her questions, for while they were trying to waken the children and hurry them off the train which stopped such a few minutes, she just smiled and vanished.

Libby and Will'm looked at each other and said in the same breath, "Miss Santa Claus!" Libby would have gone on to explain who she was, but they had reached the dining-room door, and there in the center of the breakfast table stood a Christmas tree, tipped with shining tapers and every branch a-bloom with the wonderful fruitage of Yuletide. It was the first one they had ever seen, all lighted and glistening, so it is no

OF THE PULLMAN

wonder that its glories drove everything else out of their thoughts. There was a tricycle for Will'm waiting beside his chair, with a card on it that said "With love from father and mother." And in Libby's chair with the same kind of a card was a doll, with not only real hair, but real eyelashes, and a trunk full of the most beautiful clothes that *She* had made.

As it was a holiday their father could give his entire time to making them forget that they were miles and miles from Grandma Neal and the Junction. So what with the snow fort in the yard, and a big Christmas dinner and a long sleighride afterward, they were whirled from one exciting thing to another, till nightfall. Even then there was no time to grow lonely, for their father sat in the firelight, a child on each knee, holding them close while *She* played on the piano, soft sweet lullabies so alluring that the Sandman himself had to steal out to listen.

It was different next morning when their father had to go back to the office, but the "hooking up" started out all right for Libby. She remembered it while she was washing her hands, and saw the gleam of the little new ring on her finger. So her first shy question when they were left alone with *Her,* was: "Don't you want me to do something?"

The desire to please was so evident that the answer was accompanied by a quick hug which held her close for a moment.

"Yes, dear, if you can just play with your little brother and keep him contented awhile, it will be more help than anything."

Libby skipped promptly away to do her bidding. She knew that Will'm would want to go thundering up and down the back hall in his tricycle, playing train with the lantern and the punch. She would far rather devote her time to the new doll, for she hadn't yet tried on half its wardrobe. But Miss Santa Claus's words came back to her very clearly: *"It will be like picking a little white flower whose name is obedience!"* Feeling that she was follow-

OF THE PULLMAN

ing in the footsteps of the Princess Ina, she threw herself into the game of Railroad Train until Will'm found it more thrilling than it had ever been before.

Later in the morning they trundled the tricycle out into the back yard, to ride up and down the long brick pavement which led to the alley gate. The snow had been swept off and the bricks were dry and clean. They took turns riding. The tricycle was the engine, and the one whose turn it was to go on foot ran along behind, personating the train.

They had been at this sport some time, when they suddenly became aware that some one was watching them. A small boy with curious bulging eyes, and a mouth open like a round O was peeking in at them, between the pickets of the alley gate. He was a boy two years bigger and older than Will'm, but he was unkempt looking, and his stockings wrinkled down over his shoe-tops, and there was a ring of molasses or jam or something around his mouth.

MISS SANTA CLAUS

The discovery dampened their zest in the game somewhat. It made Will'm, who had never played with any one but Libby, a trifle self-conscious. He stopped letting off steam with his lips, and wheeling around, trundled back to the house in silence. Libby, too, was disconcerted. Her car-wheels failed her. She trailed back in his wake a little girl, instead of a noisy train. Yet the discovery did not stop the game altogether. At the kitchen steps they turned as they had been doing all along and bravely started towards the alley again. This time the gate opened and the dirty little boy came in. It was Benjy, known to all the neighborhood, if not to them, for he wandered around it like a stray cat. Wherever he saw a door ajar he entered, and stayed until something attracted his attention elsewhere. He went home only when he was sent for. If nothing of interest pulled him the other way he went unresistingly, if not he was dragged. Wherever he happened to be at mealtime, he

OF THE PULLMAN

stayed, whether he was invited or not. There was something almost spooky in Benjy's sudden appearances, and in his all-devouring curiosity. It was n't the childish normal kind that asks questions. It was the gaping, uncanny kind that silently peers over into your open pocketbook, or stands looking into your mouth while you talk.

Older people disliked him because he would leave his play to stand in front of them and gape and listen, and he was always grubby and unbuttoned. Although he was six years old it was no concern of his that his stockings were always turning down over his shoe tops. If the public preferred to see them smooth then the public must attend to his gartersnaps.

The tricycle having reached the end of the walk, came to a halt. Benjy opened the gate, walked in and took possession. It was from no sense of fear that Will'm climbed down and let Benjy assume control. It was simply that a new force had come into his life, a strangely fascinating one. He

MISS SANTA CLAUS

had never had anything to do with boys before, and this one, bigger than himself, dominated him from the start. He found it much more thrilling to follow his lead than his sister's. After a few futile attempts to keep on with the game, Libby fell out of it. Not that Benjy objected to her. He simply ignored her, and Will'm took his cue from him. So she sat on the kitchen steps and watched them, till she felt cold and went into the house.

The coming of Benjy left Libby free to turn to her own affairs, but somehow she could not do it with quite the same zest, feeling that she had been shouldered out of Will'm's game by an interloper. She thoroughly disapproved of Benjy from the first glance. He was a trial to her orderly little soul, and his lack of neatness added to her resentment at being ignored. When Will'm was called in out of the cold later in the afternoon, Benjy followed as a matter of course. Several times she fell upon him and yanked him into shape with masterful

OF THE PULLMAN

touches which left him as neatly geared together as Will'm always was. But by the time he had squirmed out of her hands his gartersnaps were out of a job again, and his waist and little trousers were parting company at the belt.

All that day he stayed on, till he was dragged home at dusk like a lump of dough. He did n't resist when the maid came for him. He simply relaxed and left all the exertion of getting home entirely to her. When the door closed behind him Libby drew a long breath of relief as if she had been seven and twenty instead of just seven. He had n't *done* anything, but his wild suggestions had kept Will'm on the verge of doing things all day. He was in the act of prying the seat off his new tricycle by Benjy's orders when she went in and stopped him, and she went into the nursery just in time to keep him from doing some unheard-of thing to the radiator, so that it would blow off steam like a real engine.

Will'm had always been such a sensible

child, with a conscience of his own about injuring things, that she could n't understand why all of a sudden he should be possessed to do a hundred things that he ought not to do. It was a relief to find that the spell lifted with Benjy's removal. He came and cuddled down beside her in the big armchair before the fire, waiting for supper time to come, and somehow she felt that she had her own little brother again. He had seemed like a stranger all day. But her exile from his company had not been without its compensations.

"I can play 'Three Blind Mice! See how they run!'" she told him as they rocked back and forth. *"She* taught me. She came in while I was touching the keys just as easy, so they hardly made a sound, and asked me did I want to learn to play on them. And I said oh, yes, more than anything in the world. And she said that was exactly the way she used to feel when she was a little girl like me, living at the Junction. She wore her hair in little braids like mine and

OF THE PULLMAN

tiptoed around like a little mouse when she was in strange places, and sometimes when she looked at me she could almost believe it was her own little self come back again. Then she showed me how to make my fingers run down the keys just like the three mice did. She's going to teach me more every day till I can play it for father some night. But you must cross your heart and body not to tell 'cause I want to s'prise him."

Will'm crossed as directed, and stood by much impressed when Libby climbed up on the piano-stool and played the seven notes which she had learned, over and over: "Three blind mice! See how they run!"

"To-morrow she's going to show me as far as 'They all took after the farmer's wife.' I wish it was to-morrow right now!"

She gave an eager little wiggle that sent her slipping off the stool. "Oh, I *like* it here, now," she exclaimed, reseating herself and beginning an untiring reiteration of the seven notes.

MISS SANTA CLAUS

"So do I—some," answered Will'm. "I like it 'count of Benjy. But I don't like to hear so much blind mice. You make 'm run too long." Libby felt vaguely aggrieved by his criticism, but her pleasure in her own performance was something too great to forego.

Next morning while they were dressing, the door opened silently and Benjy appeared on Will'm's side of the screen. He came so noiselessly that it gave Libby a start when later on she was made aware of his presence. His host, equally wordless, was struggling with a little union-suit of woolen underwear. He was wordless because he was so busily occupied trying to get into it, and the unexpected entrance made him still more anxious to cover himself. Grandma Neal had always helped him with it, but he had valiantly fought off all offers of help since coming to his new home. This morning, slightly bothered by the presence of his self-invited guest, he got it so twisted that no matter how he

OF THE PULLMAN

turned it, one leg and one sleeve were always wrong side out.

Benjy, watching with his curious bulging eyes, and his mouth making a round open O, was of no more help than one of those heathen idols, who having eyes, see not, and having hands, handle not. But he finally made a suggestion. He was eager to begin playing.

"Aw, leave 'm go. Don't try to put 'em on."

It was this unexpected remark in a voice, not her brother's, which made Libby drop her button-hook, on the other side of the screen.

"But I 'll be cold," objected Will'm, staring at the strip of wintry landscape which showed through his window.

"Naw, you won't," was the confident answer. "Your outside clothes are thick."

"But I never have left them off," said Will'm, ready to cry over the exasperating tangle of legs and sleeves.

MISS SANTA CLAUS

Libby, all dressed but buttoning her shoes, heard Will'm being thus tempted of the Evil One, and peeping around the giant picture-book cover, discovered him standing in nothing but his tiny knee breeches, preparing to slip his Russian blouse of blue serge over his bare back.

"Why, Will'm Branfield! Stop this minute and put on your underclothes!" she demanded. Then growing desperate as her repeated commands were not obeyed, she called threateningly, "If you don't put them on this minute I'll tell on you."

"Huh! Who'll you tell?" jeered Benjy. "Mr. Bramfeel's down cellar, talkin' to the furnace man, and Will'm does n't have to mind *Her*. She ain't his mother."

The question gave Libby pause. Not that it left her undecided about telling, but it reminded her that she had no title to give "Her," when she called for help. It was like trying to open a door that had no knob, to call into space without having any handle of a name to take hold of first. There was

OF THE PULLMAN

no time to loose. Will'm was buttoning himself up in his blouse.

Libby hurried to the top of the stairs and called: "Sa-ay!" There was no answer, so she called again, "Sa-ay!" Then at the top of her voice, "Say! Will'm's leaving off his flannels. Please come and make him behave!"

The next instant her heart began to beat violently, and she waited in terror to see what was going to happen. She wished passionately that she had not told. Suppose she had brought down some cruel punishment on her little brother! Her first impulse had been to array herself on the side of law and order, but her second was to spread her wings like an old hen in defense of its only chick.

When *She* came into the room Will'm was backed up defiantly against the wall. She looked so pleasant and smiling as she bent over him in her pretty morning gown, that it took the courage out of him. If she had been cross he could have fought her. But

MISS SANTA CLAUS

she just stood there looking so big and capable and calm, taking it for granted that he would put on his flannels as soon as she had untwisted the funny knot they were in, that there was n't anything to do *but* obey. Will'm was a reasonable child, and if they had been alone that would have been the last of the matter. But he resented being made to mind before his company, and he resented her saying to him, "Better run on home, Benjy."

She might as well have told an oyster to run on home. He gave no sign of having heard her, and when the children went down to breakfast, he calmly went with them. He had had his, and would not sit down, but stood leaning against the table, pushing the cloth awry, watching every mouthful everybody swallowed, until Libby saw her father make a queer face. He said something to *Her* in long syllabled words, so long that only grown people could understand. And she laughed and answered that even disagreeable things might prove to be blessings

OF THE PULLMAN

in disguise, if they helped others to take root in strange places.

Benjy was dragged home again before lunch, but returned immediately after, still chewing, and bearing traces of it on both face and fingers. In the interval of his absence, "Mis' Bramfeel" as he called her, had occasion to go up-stairs. On a certain step of the stairway when her eyes were on a level with the nursery floor, she saw through its open door, something white, stuffed away back under the bureau on Will'm's side of the room. Wondering what it could be, she went in and poked it out with a cane which the boys had been playing with. To her amazement the bundle proved to be Will'm's little white union-suit. Again Libby waited with beating heart and clasped hands while he was called in and buttoned firmly into it. *She* forbade him sternly not to take it off again till bedtime, but nothing else happened, and Libby breathed freely once more. Grandma Neal would have spanked him she thought. Will'm needed spanking now and then if one could only be sure that it would n't be done too hard.

Mr. Branfield did not come home till late that night. He was called out of town on business. As soon as the telephone message came, *She* gave the cook a holiday, and told Libby she was going to get supper herself. Libby could choose whatever she and Will'm liked best, and they'd surprise him with it after Benjy had been dragged home. So Libby chose, and was left to keep house while *She* hurried down to the only place in town where she was sure of getting what Libby had chosen, and carried it home herself, and cooked it just as they used to cook them at the Junction when she was a little girl and lived there years ago. And Libby had the best time helping. As she followed *Her* about the kitchen she thought of the things she intended to tell Maudie Peters the first time they went back to the Junction to visit.

She and Libby talked a great deal about that prospective visit, for *She* had made

OF THE PULLMAN

playhouses under the same old thorn-tree by the brook where Libby's last one was. And she had coasted down Clifford hill many a time, and she had even sat in the third seat from the front in the row next to the western wall, one whole term of school. That was Libby's own seat. No wonder she knew just how Libby felt about everything when she could remember so many experiences that were like this little girl's who followed her back and forth from table to stove, bringing up all her own childhood before her.

Will'm sniffed expectantly as he climbed up to the supper table. A delicious and a beloved odor had reached him. He smiled like a full moon when his plate was put in front of him, and his spoon went hurriedly up to his mouth. "Oh, rabbit *dravy!*" he sighed ecstatically.

She had gone back to the kitchen for something else, and Libby took occasion to say reprovingly, "Yes, and *She* went a long, long way to get that rabbit, just because I

MISS SANTA CLAUS

told her you love 'm so. And *She* cooked it herself and burned her hand a-doing it. *She* was gathering a star-flower for you, even if you have been bad and forgot what Miss Santa Claus told you!"

When *She* came back with the rest of the supper, Will'm stole a glance at her hands. Sure enough, one was bound up in a handkerchief. It had not been blistered by nettles, but it had been blistered for him. Hastily swallowing what was in his spoon, he slid down from the table.

"Why, what's the matter, dear?" she asked in surprise. "Don't you like it after all?"

He cast one furtive, abashed look at her as he sidled towards the door. There was confession in that look, and penitence and a sturdy resolve to make what atonement he could. Then from the hall he called back the rather enigmatical answer, "I have n't *got* 'em on, but I'm going to *put* 'em on!" And the "rabbit dravy" waited while he clattered up the stairs to wriggle

OF THE PULLMAN

out of his suit and into the flannels, which Benjy's jeers had made him discard just before supper, for the third time that day.

CHAPTER VII

IN the story it was six long years before the Princess Ina completed her task, but less than a week went by before Libby was convinced that the charm was a potent one, and that Miss Santa Claus had spoken truly. But there was one thing she could not understand. In the story, one found the star-flowers only among nettles and briars, and gathered them to the accompaniment of scratches and stings. Yet she was finding it not only a pleasure to obey this new authority but a tingling happiness to do anything for her which would call forth some smile of approval or a caress.

Still, she saw that the story way was the true way in Will'm's case, for so many things that he was told to do, made him feel all "cross and scratchy and hot." They interfered with his play or clashed with the ideas

MISS SANTA CLAUS

he imbibed from Benjy. Some of Benjy's ideas were as "catching" and distorting as the mumps.

The conductor's punch did not long continue to be the daily reminder to Will'm that Libby's ring was to her, for it mysteriously disappeared one day, and was lost for months. It disappeared the very day that a row of little star-shaped holes was found along the edge of the expensive Holland window-shade in the front window of the parlor. Benjy had suggested punching them. He wanted a lot of little stars to paste all over their shoes. Why he wanted them nobody but he could understand.

But the punch served its purpose, for the Holland shade was not taken down on account of the holes, and whenever the row of little stars met Molly Branfield's eyes, they reminded her of the day when Libby threw herself into her arms, calling her "Mother" for the first time, and sobbing out the story of Ina and the swans. Distressed by Will'm's wickedness, Libby begged her not to stop loving him even if he did keep on being naughty, and to try the charm on him which would change him into a real little son. Many a time in the months which followed, the row of little holes brought a smile of tolerant tenderness, when she was puzzling over ways to deal with the stubbornness of the small boy who resented her authority. She knew that it was not because he was bad that he resented it, but because, as Libby suggested, he had "started out wrong in his hooking-up." Many a time Libby was moved to say mournfully, "Oh, if he'd just remembered what Miss Santa Claus told him, this never would have happened!"

It was not every day, however, that this crookedness was apparent. Often from daylight till dark he went happily from one thing to another, without a single incident to mar the peacefulness of the hours. He liked the new home with its banisters to slide down, and its many windows looking out on streets where something interesting was al-

OF THE PULLMAN

ways happening. He liked to water the flowers in the dining-room windows. It made him feel that he was helping make a spot of summertime in the world, when all out of doors was white with snow. One of the pots of flowers was his, a rose-geranium. Even before the wee buds began to swell, it was a thing of joy, for he had only to rub his fingers over a leaf to make it send forth a smell so good that one longed to eat it.

He liked the race down the hall every evening trying to beat Libby to the door to open it for their father. Now that he was acquainted with him again, it seemed the very nicest thing in the world to have a big jolly father who could swing him up on his shoulder and play circus tricks with him just like an acrobat, and who knew fully as much as the president of the United States.

And Will'm liked the time which often came before that race down the hall—the wait in the firelight, while *She* played on the piano and he and Libby sang with her. There was one song about the farmer feeding his flocks, "with a quack, quack here, and a gobble, gobble there," that he liked especially. Whenever they came to the chorus of the flocks and the herds it was such fun to make all the barnyard noises. Sometimes with their lusty mooing and lowing the noise would be so great that they would fail to hear the latchkey turn in the door, and first thing they knew there their father would be in the room mooing with them, in a deep voice that thrilled them like a bass drum.

Libby entered school after the holidays, and Benjy started back on his second half-year, but he did not go regularly. Many a day when he should have been in his classes, he was playing War in the Branfield attic, or Circus in the nursery. It was always on those days that the crookedness of Will'm was more manifest, and for that reason, a great effort was made periodically to get rid of Benjy. But it seemed a hopeless task. He might be set bodily out of doors and told to go home, but even locks and

OF THE PULLMAN

bolts could not keep him out. He oozed in again somewhere, just like smoke. Repeated telephone messages to his mother had no effect. She seemed as indifferent to his being a nuisance to the neighbors as he was to his gartersnaps being unfastened. Several times, thinking to escape him when he had announced his intention the night before of coming early, Mrs. Branfield took Will'm down town with her, shopping. But he trailed them around the streets just like a little dog till he found them, and attached himself as joyously as if they had whistled to him. And he looked even worse than an unwashed, uncombed little terrier, for he was always unbuttoned and ungartered besides.

Upon these appearances, Will'm, who a moment before had been the most interested and interesting of companions, pointing at the shop windows and asking questions in a high, happy little voice, would pull loose from his companion's hand and fall back beside Benjy. The worst of it was that the

MISS SANTA CLAUS

unwelcome visitor rarely did anything that could be pointed out to Will'm as an offense. It was simply that his presence had a subtle, moving quality like yeast, which started fermentation in the Branfield household whenever he dropped into it.

Fortunately, when summer came, Benjy's mother departed to the seashore, taking him with her, and Will'm made the acquaintance of the children on the next block. There were several boys his own size who swarmed in the Branfield yard continually. He had a tent for one thing, which was an unusual attraction, and a slide. Up to a reasonable point he had access to a cooky jar and an apple barrel. Often, little tarts found their way to the tent on mornings when "the gang" proposed playing elsewhere, and often the long hot afternoons were livened with pitchers of lemonade in which ice clinked invitingly; a nice big chunk apiece, which lasted till the lemonade was gone, and could be used afterward in a sort of game. You dropped them on the ground to see who

OF THE PULLMAN

could pick his up and hold it the longest with his bare toes.

Will'm had a birthday about this time, with five candles on his cake and five boys, besides Libby, to share the feast. He loved all these things. He was proud of having treats to offer the boys which they could not find in any other yard on that street, and in time he began to love the hand which dealt them out. He might have done so sooner if Libby had not been so aggravating about it. She always took occasion to tell him afterward that such kindnesses were the little golden star-flowers mother was gathering for him, and that he ought to be ashamed to do even the littlest thing she told him not to, when she was so good to him.

Unfortunately Libby had overheard her mother speak of her as a real little comfort in the way she tried to uphold her authority and help her manage Will'm. The remark made her doubly zealous and her efforts, in consequence, doubly offensive to Will'm. He was learning early that a saint is one

MISS SANTA CLAUS

of the most exasperating people in the world to live with. Even when they don't *say* anything, they can make you feel the contrast sometimes so strongly that you *want* to be bad on purpose, just because they are the way they are.

Libby's little ring still turned her waking thoughts in the direction of Ina and the swans, and her morning remarks usually pointed the same way. The cherry-red stocking with its tinsel fringe hung from the side of her mirror, the most cherished ornament in the room, and a daily reminder of Miss Santa Claus, who was forever enshrined in her little heart as one of the dearest memories of her life. She felt that she owed everything to Miss Santa Claus. But for her she might have started out crooked, and might never have found her way to the mother-love which had grown to be such a precious thing to her that she could not bear for Will'm not to share it fully with her.

He learned to fight that summer, and nothing made him quite so furious as to have

OF THE PULLMAN

Libby interfere when he had some boy down, and by sheer force of will it seemed, since her three years' advantage in age gave her little in strength, pull him off his adversary, flapping and scratching like a little gamecock. Sometimes it made him so angry that he wanted to tear her in pieces. The worst of it was, that *She* always took Libby's part on such occasions, and never seemed to understand that it was necessary for him to do these things. She always looked so sorry and worried when he was dragged into the house, roaring and resentful.

Gradually as summer wore on into the autumn, it began to make him feel uncomfortable when he saw that sorry, worried look. It hurt him worse than when she sent him to his room or tied him to the table leg for punishment. And one night when he had openly defied her and been impudent, she did not say anything, but she did not kiss him good-night as usual. That hurt him worst of all. He lay awake a long time thinking about it. Part of the time he was crying softly, but he had his face snuggled close down in the pillow so that Libby could n't hear him.

He wished with all his heart that she was his own, real mother. He felt that he needed one. He needed one who could *understand* and who had a *right* to punish him. It was because she had n't that right that he resented her authority. All the boys said she had n't. If she did no more than call from the window: "Don't do that, Will'm," they 'd say in an undertone, "You don't have to pay any attention to *her!*" They seemed to think it was all right for their mothers to slap them and scold them and cuff them on the ears. He 'd seen it done. He would n't care how much he was slapped and cuffed, if only somebody who was his truly *own* did it. Somebody who loved him. A queer little feeling had been creeping up in his heart for some time. Very often when *She* spoke to Libby she called her "little daughter" and she and Libby seemed to belong to each other in a way that

OF THE PULLMAN

shut Will'm out and gave him a lonesome left-in-the-cold feeling. Will'm was a reasonable child, and he was just, and up there in the dark where he could be honest with himself, he had to acknowledge that it was his own fault that she had n't kissed him good-night. It was his fault because, having started out crooked, he did n't seem to be able to do anything but to go on crooked to the end. He could n't tell her, but he wished, oh, how he wished, that *She* could know how he felt, and know that he was crying up there in the dark about it. He wished he could go back to the Junction and be Grandma Neal's little boy. She always kissed him good-night, even on days when she had to switch him with a peach-tree switch. When he was a little bigger he would just run off and go back to Grandma Neal.

But next morning he was glad that he was not living at the Junction, for he started to kindergarten, and a world of new interests opened up before him. Benjy came back to town that week, but he did not find quite the same tractable follower. Will'm had learned how to play with other boys, and how to make other boys do *his* bidding, so he did not always allow Benjy to dictate. Still the leaven of an uneasy presence began working again, and worked on till it was suddenly counteracted by the coming of another Christmas season.

Both Libby and Will'm began to feel its approach when it was still a month off. They felt it in the mysterious thrills that began to stir the household as sap, rising in a tree, thrills it with stirrings of spring. There were secrets and whisperings. There was counting of pennies and planning of ways to earn more, for they were wiser about Christmas this year. They knew that there are three kinds of presents. There is the kind that Santa Claus puts into your stocking, just because he *is* Santa Claus, and the Sky Road leads from his Kingdom of Giving straight to the kingdom of little hearts who love and believe in him.

OF THE PULLMAN

Then there's the kind that you give to the people you love, just because you love them, and you put your name on those. And third, there's the kind that you give secretly, in the name of Santa Claus, just to help him out if he is extra busy and should happen to send you word that he needs your services.

Libby and Will'm received no such messages, being so small, but their father had one. He sent a load of coal and some rent money to a man who had lost a month's wages on account of sickness in his family, and it must have been a very happy and delightful feeling that Santa Claus gave their father for doing it, for his voice sounded that way afterward when he said, "After all, Molly, that's the best kind of giving. We ought to do more of it and less of the other."

When it came to the first kind of presents, neither Libby nor Will'm made a choice. They sent their names and addresses up the chimney so that the reindeer

MISS SANTA CLAUS

might be guided to the right roof-top, and left the rest to the generosity of the reindeer's wise master to surprise them as he saw fit. They were almost sure that the things they daily expressed a wish for would come by the way of the Christmas tree as the doll and the tricycle had the year before, "with the love of father and mother."

But when it came to the second kind of presents, they had much to consider. They wanted to give to the family and each other, and the cook and their teachers, and the children they played with most and half a dozen people at the Junction. The visit which they had planned all year was to be a certainty now. The day after Christmas the entire family was to go for a week's visit, to Grandma and Uncle Neal.

That last week the children went around the house in one continual thrill of anticipation. Such delicious odors of popcorn and boiling candy, of cake and mincemeat in the making floated up from the kitchen! Such rustling of tissue paper and scent of sachets

OF THE PULLMAN

as met one on the opening of bureau drawers! And such rapt moments of gift-making when Libby sewed with patient, learning fingers, and Will'm pasted paper chains and wove paper baskets, as he had been taught in kindergarten!

One day the conductor's punch suddenly reappeared, and he seized it with a whoop of joy. Now all his creations could be doubly beautiful since they could be star-bordered. As he punched and punched and the tiny stars fell in a shower, the story of Ina and the swans stirred in his memory, with all the glamour it had worn when he first heard it over his dish of strawberries. Down in his secret soul he determined to do what he wished he had done a year earlier, to begin to follow the example of Ina.

The family could not fail to notice the almost angelic behavior which began that day. They thought it was because of the watching eye he feared up the chimney, but no one referred to the change. He used to sit in front of the fire sometimes, just as he had done at the Junction, rocking and singing, his soft bobbed hair flapping over his ears every time the rockers tilted forward. But he was not singing with any thought that he might be overheard and written down as a good little boy. He was singing just because the story of the Camels and the Star was so very sweet, and the mere thought of angels and silver bells and the glittering Sky Road brought a tingling joy. But more than all he was singing because he had begun to weave the big beautiful mantle whose name is Love, and the curious little left-out-in-the-cold feeling was gone.

Christmas eve came at last. When the twilight was just beginning to fall, Libby brought down the stockings which were to be hung on each side of the sitting-room fireplace. It would be nearly an hour before their father could come home to drive the nails on which they were to hang, but they wanted everything ready for him. Will'm went out to the tool-chest on the

OF THE PULLMAN

screened porch to get the hammer. It took him a long time to find it.

Libby waited impatiently a few moments, supposing he had stopped to taste something in the kitchen. She was about to run out and warn him not to nip the edges from some tempting bit of pastry, as he had been known to do, but remembering how very hard he had been trying to be good all week, she decided he could be trusted.

With the stockings thrown over one arm she stood in front of the piano, idly striking the keys while she waited. She had learned to play several tunes during the year, and now that she was eight years old, she was going to have real lessons after the holidays and learn to read music. How much she had learned since the first time her little fingers were guided over the keys. She struck those earliest-learned notes again: "Three blind mice! See how they run!" She could play the whole thing now, faster than flying. She ran down the keys, over and over again.

When for about the twentieth time "they

MISS SANTA CLAUS

all took after the farmer's wife," she stopped short, both hands lifted from the keys to listen. Her face blanched until even her lips were pale. Such a sound of awful battle was coming from the back yard! Recognizing Will'm's voice she ran out through the kitchen to the yard.

"It's that everlastin' Benjy, again!" called the cook as Libby darted out the door to rescue Will'm from she knew not what.

But it was Benjy who needed rescuing this time. Will'm sat on top, so mighty in his wrath and fury that he loomed up fearsomely to the bigger boy beneath him, whose body he bestrode and whose face he was battering with hard and relentless little fists. Both boys were blubbering and crying, but Will'm was roaring between blows, "Take it back! Take it back!"

Whatever it was, Benjy took it back just as Libby appeared, and being allowed to stagger up, started for the street, loudly boo-hooing at every step, as he found his way homeward, for once of his own volition.

"Take it back!"

OF THE PULLMAN

The cries had startled Libby but they were as nothing to the sight that met her eyes when she led Will'm, so blinded by his own tears that he needed her guidance, to the light of the kitchen door. What she saw sent her screaming into the house, with agonized calls for "mother." She still held on to Will'm's hand, pulling him along after her.

From forehead to chin, one side of his face was scratched as if a young tiger cat had set his claws in it. A knot was swelling rapidly on his upper lip, and one hand was covered with blood. Mrs. Branfield gave a gasp as she came running in answer to Libby's calls. "Why, you poor child!" she cried, gathering him up to her and sitting down in the big rocker with him in her lap. "What happened? What's the matter?"

He was sobbing so convulsively now, with long choking gasps, that he couldn't answer. She saw that his face was only scratched, but snatched up his hand to examine the extent of its injuries. As he

MISS SANTA CLAUS

looked at it too, the power of speech came back to him, in a degree.

"That is n't m-my b-blood!" he sobbed. "It's *B-Benjy's* blood!"

"Oh, Will'm!" mourned Libby. "On Christmas eve, just when you 've been trying so hard to be good, too!"

She picked up the stockings which she had dropped on running out of the house, and laid his over the back of a chair, as if she realized the hopelessness of hanging it up now, after he had acted so. At that, almost a spasm of sobs shook him. He did n't need anybody to remind him of all he had forfeited and all he had failed in. That was what he was crying about. He did n't mind the smarting of his face or the throbbing of his swollen lip. He was crying to think that the struggle of the last week was all for naught. He was all crooked with *Her* again. *She* did n't want him to fight and she 'd never understand that this time he just *had* to.

The arms that held him were pressing for

OF THE PULLMAN

an answer. "Tell me how it happened, dear."

Between gulps it came.

"Benjy said for me to come on—and go to the grocery with him! And I said—that my—my mother—did n't want me to!"

"Yes," encouragingly, as he choked and stopped. He had never called her that before.

"And Benjy said like he always does, that you w-was n't my m-m-mother anyhow. And I said you *was!* If he did n't take it back I—*I'd beat him up!*"

Libby was crying too, now, from sympathy. He'd been told so many times he must not fight that she was afraid he would have to be punished for such a bad fight as this. To be punished on Christmas eve was just *too* awful! She stole an anxious glance towards the chimney, then toward her mother.

But her mother was hugging him tight and kissing him wherever she could find a place on his poor little face that was n't scratched or swollen, and she was saying in a voice that made a lump come into Libby's throat, it was so loving and tender,

"My dear little boy, if that's why you fought him I'm *glad* you did it, for you've proved now that you *are* my little son, my very own!"

Then she laughed, although she had tears in her eyes herself, and said, "That poor little cheek shows just what fierce nettles and briars you've been through for me, but you brought it, didn't you! The most precious star-flower in all the world to me!"

The surprise of it stopped his tears. She *understood!* He could not yet stop the sobbing. That kept on, doing itself. But a feeling, warm and tender that he could not explain, seemed to cover him "from wing-tip to wing-tip!" A bloody little hand stole up around her neck and held her tight. She *was* his mother, because she *understood!* It was all right between them now. It would *always* be all right, no matter what Benjy and the rest of the world might say. He'd

OF THE PULLMAN

beat up anybody that dared to say they did n't belong to each other, and she *wanted* him to do it!

Presently she led him up-stairs to put some healing lotion on his face, and wash away the blood of Benjy.

Libby, in the deep calm that followed the excitement of so many conflicting emotions, sat down in the big rocking chair to wait for her father. Her fear for Will'm had been so strong, her relief at the happy outcome so great, that she felt all shaken up. A long, long time she sat there, thinking. There was only one more thing needed to make her happiness complete, and that was to have Miss Santa Claus know that the charm had worked out true at last. She felt that they owed her that much—to let her know. Presently she slipped out of the chair and knelt in front of the fire so close that it almost singed her.

"Are you listening up there?" she called softly. " 'Cause if you are, *please* tell Miss Santa Claus that everything turned out just as she said it would. I'll be *so* much obliged."

Then she scudded back to her chair to listen for her father's latchkey in the door, and her mother's and Will'm's voices coming down the stairs, a happier sound than even the sound of the silver bells, that by and by would come jingling down the Sky Road.

THE END